DEAR ARTHUR,

THE FRUITS OF YOUR LABOUR

SYLVIA ANNE HOSKINS

Elvira Publishing

Published and distributed by: Elvira Publishing,
Craigshannoch Lodge, Midmar, Inverurie, Aberdeenshire,
Scotland, AB51 7LX.

Cover design: Lucy Wilson, Woolly Pig Paintings,
www.sites.google.com/site/woollypigpaintings

Interior Illustration of Arthur McCluskey: Tibor Devic

ISBN - 978-0-9927811-0-1

To buy this book: Elvirapublishing@aol.com

Printed in Ireland by:
iSupply Ltd. Unit 4, Glenrock Business Park,
Ballybane Industrial Estate, Galway, Ireland.
Tel: 00353 91 755705
www.isupplyonline.com

DEDICATION

I dedicate this book to,
Our Blessed Mother in Heaven
and to the people of
Bosnia and Herzegovina

Not, How did he Die, but How did he Live?

Not, how did he die, but how did he live?
Not, what did he gain, but what did he give?
These are the units to measure the worth
Of a man as a man, regardless of birth.
Not what was his church, nor what was his creed?
But had he befriended those really in need?
Was he ever ready, with words of good cheer,
To bring back a smile, to banish a tear?
Not what did the sketch in the newspaper say,
But how many were sorry when he passed away?

Anonymous

CONTENTS

Acknowledgements

Foreword   -   Fr. Svetozar Kraljevic, OFM.

ACKNOWLEDGEMENTS

When Arthur, Lisa my stepdaughter and I travelled on that road to Kiseljak in November 2010, little did I know that the 'book for the future' which we were discussing, would be written and published after Arthur's death. Arthur was always such a 'larger than life' type figure, so I had never anticipated that our dear friend would leave us to go home to God much earlier than any of us expected. I am therefore grateful to the help of the following people for bringing to fruition the book which Arthur, Lisa and I had discussed and planned and without whom this book would not have been brought to its completion.

First to Arthur's sister, Pat Henry, Chairman of St. Joseph & the Helpers Charity (UK), I thank you for your encouragement in writing the book and for your critical eye. Your school teaching skills have come into their own as you have trawled through grammatical error and factual information. I am deeply grateful for your time, your commitment and for the laughter and tears which we have shared as the book unfolded. Your friendship is a treasured gift.

I thank Arthur's close friend Donal O'Shea, Director of St Joseph & The Helpers (UK). Donal worked closely with Arthur in identifying the many projects which have now come to fruition. Donal's knowledge of the charity is unequivocal and the information which he gave me has been invaluable; Donal helped me to put flesh on the bones of the book and so it is to his credit that I have written the book with detail and accuracy as Arthur would have wanted. I am sure your telephone bill has increased significantly in the past two years. Arthur will be laughing.

To Lisa Nicholls, my step-daughter, who painstakingly took notes as we travelled and interviewed the many people mentioned in this book. Lisa, you are redeemed; your note-taking gave me the skeleton for the book and was invaluable in the days when I searched for detail, or where the voice-recordings were unclear. Thank you for your patience with this difficult task.

Throughout the journey of researching and writing the book, I interviewed many people who were the beneficiaries of Arthur's generosity, his tireless spirit and his compassion. They gave me hours of their precious time and shared many beautiful memories with me.

I thank therefore the Franciscan Priests in Visoko, Fr Franjo Radman and Fr Josip; in Medjugorje, Fr Svetozar; Fr Slavisa in Dezevice; in Sarajevo, Fr. Pero, Fr Šimo. I am also grateful for Fr. Mijo Dzolan's input. He had been moved from Visoko by the time we were researching the material but he managed to give me information and insight when we met at the "Seminar: Addiction to Gambling – between Illness and Personal-Social Responsibility" in Medjugorje, October 2012, where I had the opportunity to give a lecture on Arthur's conversion from gambling.

I am grateful for the help of the Franciscan Sisters in Kiseljak: Sr Jelenka, Sr Lidija, Sr Ana, Sr Kata, Sr Valerijana, Sr Ivana, Sr Marijana; in Bjele Polje: Sr Dominika and Sr Marija.. In Vionica, Rosa Stojic, Sr Kornelije's niece stepped in to help with the introductions and interpretations. Thank you Rosa for your generous gift of time. Thank you also to Sr Janja for sharing with me over a cup of coffee in Medjugorje. Arthur always had a great deal of love and respect for you and I am grateful for your time.

I was deeply moved by the work in Miracles centre and I thank Mathew Procter for his time and patience in explaining to me all the wonderful projects going on at the centre. I asked Mathew to help me find a mini-bus, driver and interpreter and he came up trumps with Adem Dugalic and Adnan Safro from Mostar. Adem's driving gave me great comfort as he negotiated the twisted and turning mountain roads and Adnan was a wonderful interpreter who made life so much easier on our journey. Thank you both very much. When we drove to Visoko we met Florence Graham, an American teacher who spoke Croatian fluently, and who did a wonderful job at interpreting between us all and giving a personal insight into the work of the Franciscans at Visoko. Florence also contributed to the book some personal reflections on her time at Visoko. Thank you, Florence; you are a delight and an excellent communicator.

When Jane Dowd took Lisa and me with her to visit some of the people she helps, as fellow nurses we were deeply moved at the conditions of many sick people and the wonderful work undertaken by Jane's nurses from St. Luke's Homecare. Thank you for your time, Jane. You are an inspiration to us all.

Hospitality comes in many forms, but none as beautiful as that given by Vesna Radišić, owner of 'Pansion St. Michael' in Medjugorje. Thank you Vesna for your wonderful memories of Arthur, your delicious coffee and cakes and for respite from the world in your warm and welcoming home. Arthur came to life when you talked of him and without you many of the poorest of the poor would have been overlooked. Thank you for your time and commitment to this book, to Arthur and to the people.

I thank Miljenka Majic for organising a place for me to stay at Mother's Village in May 2013. This gave me the opportunity to complete much of the writing of this book. Miljenka is a great net-worker and through her I have met many people. Thank you Miljenka for your friendship and help in assisting me to complete the task.

Raymond McGreevy was responsible for introducing me to Arthur and I am grateful for that experience in my life and through Arthur,

Michael Douglas and I met. Thank you Michael and your lovely wife Lily, for proof-reading the book and making some very good suggestions. Thank you also to Tea Susac, a wonderful translator and friend.

The one theme that consistently came through when I talked to many people in Bosnia and Herzegovina was their gratitude for all the help given to them through Arthur and his charity. In many cases, this was the difference between life and death; in others, the difference between having hope and losing hope; but in every case there was a story of the struggle to survive. I am in awe at the gentle, dignified, quiet strength of the people and I thank them for sharing their experiences with me.

Finally, I thank Lucy Wilson, my niece, from 'Woolly Pig Paintings' for designing the front and back covers of this book; Lisa Nicholls for taking the photograph of Arthur, Fr Slavisa, Sr Lidija and me in Kiseljak; Mary Killeen for contributing her photograph of Arthur, Fr Svet and Donal O'Shea at the 'Night of the Dogs' in March 2008; Pat Henry for contributing the photographs of Cardinal Vinko Puljic and Arthur; The Family Picture and the Public Kitchen in Sarajevo. All the other photographs in this book, including the photograph of the fig tree were taken by me. I do not claim to be a photographer but I hope I have captured the essence of Arthur's work. I thank Tibor Devic for contributing the sketch of Arthur for this book. It is extremely well done and captures the 'real' Arthur perfectly.

And so to Arthur. We owe much to that gentle giant and I cannot finish without saying that in life we meet some people who will remain in our hearts forever. Arthur is one of those people and I thank him for a wonderful journey as I accompanied him in his charity work in Bosnia and Herzegovina. He and my husband, Rick did not talk much, but they spoke their common language as they prayed the Rosary together.

With that, I must thank Our Blessed Mother for the intricate tapestry which she wove through Arthur McCluskey.

Sylvia Anne Hoskins

November 2013.

Foreword

Arthur did see hell. He saw it in the lonely days and nights looking at dogs and horses racing to bring him consolation, just to be able to crawl to the next day. Reaching into the glasses filled with alcohol Arthur was trying to control the body and the spirit in it, when every other way failed.

In a mysterious way, at the moment chosen by God the heavenly grace intervened and Arthur 's life changed. At that moment the life of Arthur and consequently the lives of many changed for time and for eternity.

Arthur's Mother was always there. A friend gave him a simple rosary. Mr. Joe McFadden asked him to come on pilgrimage. Arthur allowed the risk. The flight to Medjugorje, the providential encounter with fellow pilgrims led him into unknown territory of prayer and faith.

A sense of fear comes with the thought: What if this pilgrimage and conversion did not take place. What would be the destiny of Arthur's life? Where the lives of so many would have gone?

When Arthur climbed the mountain of Križevac he himself became a mountain of God. In his conversion he received faith both in God and in Man. Out of that faith kindergartens and homes for poor, playgrounds for children were built. His own life, the body and the soul, became the refuge for all those who needed him.

In that moment when Arthur said YES to the heavenly grace he became ready to receive the sacraments and all the miracles that God wanted to give to him and through him till the end of his life.

His acceptance of this irrational Medjugorje pilgrimage, which was far beyond his understanding and totally opposed to his ways indicates the drama of the journey he made.   His surrender to the call gently   reminds us of Mary listening to Angel Gabriel.

I wonder when did those monuments of love in Kiseljak, in Tomislavgrad, in Mostar, at Mother's Village in Medjugorje were made.   Not when the builders were pouring out the cement, not when the bricks were laid one upon the other and not when the people were able to take picture of the finished buildings. They were built at those moments of grace when Arthur became ready for Jesus and Mary.   Then   Jesus and Mary were ready to use him and to change the face of the earth in many ways.

Once I came to Dublin to be present at a special event, which Arthur organized to help one of his projects in Bosnia and Herzegovina. Great number of people was present. Arthur and myself (me in our Franciscan habit) were   walking from table to table. The way people listened to Arthur impressed me very much.   Then a little later without Arthur I went to speak with people.   Soon I realized they did not even notice me. Arthur had a charisma of the word and a presence that captured their hearts.   People were able to see and recognize the greatness of a man that he was.

Conversion of one will always bring the grace to many. When horses and dogs were stopped, when prayer started flowing Arthur became an instrument for the Words and the Works of God. All of us who knew Arthur saw in him a witness, a new biblical story in our time.

Now Arthur does appear dead but the children in the kindergarten in Kiseljak, children at Mother's Village in Medjugorje, those people who changed their lives because of his testimony see and feel him very much alive and present. Those who will read these pages will be gently challenged by his ways and called.

Fr Svetozar Kraljevic, O.F.M.

November 2013

INTRODUCTION

Arthur McCluskey

by Sylvia Hoskins

When I first met Arthur, I could not help but notice three things about him: his twinkling eyes, his shy, lopsided grin, and his shoes which looked as if they had never encountered a lick of polish at any time in their lives. "You can tell a man by his shoes" goes the saying and they are right; for eighteen hours a day, seven days a week, those shoes carried the weight of a tall ex-rugby player, taking him through dusty streets, mud-tracked mountains and desolate refugee camps in Bosnia and Herzegovina. They endured the scraping of hard concrete floors as Arthur knelt in prayer, pleading God for help, imploring him to send the funds that would be needed for the work to be done. They were neglected shoes, but tough, like their owner, faithfully trudging through the terrain of a war-torn land to bring sustenance and hope to a destitute people who had endured a brutal conflict from 1992-1995 which came about as a result of the break-up of the Socialist Federal Republic of Yugoslavia. It was principally a territorial conflict, involving Serb forces, Bosniak Muslims and Croat forces.   In the resulting conflict approximately 100,000 people were killed and over 2,000,000 people displaced.

At the end of each day, Arthur's shoes suffered the humiliation of being kicked off without ceremony as their exhausted owner collapsed into bed and, first thing in the morning they suffered

1

the anonymity of being ignored as Arthur leapt to the call of prayer. Arthur's shoes were heroic in their endeavour to keep this driven man standing safely, through all weather, throughout the year, but they were tired and eventually like their owner, longed for the respite that would come sooner than expected.

Background

Arthur McCluskey was born in Ireland in 1944. He was the seventh child of eight children; six sisters and an older brother. His family were traditional Irish Catholics, praying the Rosary every evening and attending Mass. Arthur had a good childhood brought up by solid hard-working parents but in 1956, at the age of twelve years, Arthur placed his first gambling bet on the English Grand National and to his delight his horses won first and second in the race. The success of this win was to convince Arthur that this was as an easy way to make money and planted the seed of a habit that would, later on in his life, bring him to the point of near personal destruction.

In 1964, seeking the opportunities of a post-war Britain, Arthur emigrated to Scotland. He was nineteen years old, naïve about the way of the world and business, but willing to work hard and by the time he was twenty-seven years of age, in 1971, he had set up his own furniture business. He was a hard worker and in some ways quite ruthless, but he became very successful financially and according to his own testimony, led a wonderful hedonistic life-style, spending money freely on whatever he desired.

By 1974, Arthur owned his own racehorses and within a very short time, those horses won thirty major races in the United Kingdom (UK) and Ireland. Costing thousands of pounds sterling, he travelled with his racehorses on Jumbo Jets taking them to races all over the world. He himself was a frequent flyer on Concorde, travelling to exotic places throughout the world. He had money 'to burn' and from his perception, he had everything in life.

Arthur's Goal

Arthur's goal in life was to make money because, from his point of view, money was the key to happiness. Happiness was also horses; he loved horses for their grace and elegance, but also because they could potentially win races and make him more money. Happiness also included alcohol, especially champagne and Arthur led what he would refer to as a 'champagne life-style': selfish, self-indulgent and without too much thought for others.

In order to make more money to fund his horses, Arthur turned to gambling on horses, often winning, but more often losing. Within a very short time, Arthur became a compulsive gambler and for the next twenty years, he focused on gambling his money by placing bets on horses, often losing over £30,000 per day.

The Habit

How did Arthur develop this habit? First, there was 'a goal' which was to make money; then, 'the illusion' that gambling gave him the opportunity to make more money quickly. This was followed by 'self-deception'. Gambling venues welcomed him and treated him as a special guest which in turn increased his self-esteem. He enjoyed feeling special so his frequent visits to betting shops became a 'routine'. Every day Arthur gambled because he wanted to make more money and he enjoyed feeling very special and important. In addition Arthur had plenty of money with which to fund his gambling habit and in fact he never quite reached the bottom where he would be ruined financially. In time, he became comfortable in the familiar environment of the gambling venue.

Addiction

Like all addictions, his addiction to gambling was a gradual process and in the environment of gambling where winning or losing could happen, alcohol became the partner with gambling. When his horses won, he became exhilarated and he gambled more; when his horses lost, he felt he had to gamble to try and win the money back again. The more he lost, the more he panicked and felt desperate. He then felt helpless if he continued to lose. Gambling became such a compulsion, that on Saturday afternoons, if he were not at the races, he would go home, sit in his rocking chair and watch the races on television. His telephone would be primed on the redial mode and he would phone his 'bookies' (bookmakers), placing bets right up to the last race, at the last minute of the racing day. His gambling brought him to near personal ruin and destroyed his business, with the loss of one hundred jobs, the entire workforce.

The Illness

Gambling had a negative effect on Arthur's well-being: psychologically, physically, socially and spiritually. Although he appeared unaware of how ill he was, gradually, Arthur's health deteriorated.

Psychologically, he suffered from an undiagnosed depression but always pretended to be cheerful, always smiling. He experienced tremendous guilt, unable to control his secretive gambling, wasting so much precious money, always remembering the struggles of his parents when he was younger and unable to face his mother who was alive at that time. In addition Arthur felt remorse for wasting money, for being secretive, vowing to himself that he would change his ways that he could control his gambling, but his financial situation worsened and he was unable to control his compulsions resulting in dark moods, arrogance, being difficult and argumentative.

Physically, the more depressed Arthur become, the more he drowned his depression in alcohol. His fine taste for champagne exacerbated his financial situation, but helped him to alleviate the pain of failure. His eating habits were poor and he deprived his body of essential vitamins resulting in morning shakes, sweating profusely and feeling as if he were having a heart attack. He had neither the will nor energy to exercise and his weight, fat layers, and breathlessness on exertion increased significantly.

Socially, Arthur became secretive; feeling ashamed of his gambling habit and massive loss of money. He lied about where he had been and what he was doing. Arthur never married, but had a close relationship with a good woman for nearly eighteen years. Since they lived in separate houses, she did not know his whereabouts, but at one time suspected that he might be having an affair with another woman. Little did she realise that the "other woman" was gambling. Eventually, Arthur was arrested for driving whilst being over the legal alcohol limit and his driving licence was removed from him legally for long periods of time. Once he spent a night in the police cells, totally inebriated, unable to function.

Spiritually, Arthur rejected the Christian/Catholic faith which he had known since childhood and stopped attending Church except on the occasions when his mother would visit him in Glasgow and he would accompany her to Mass.[1] He perceived God as being old-fashioned and irrelevant and Arthur's viewpoint was that he was in control of his own life, that he was a successful businessman and he did not need God.

The Happenings: Love

Although Arthur had rejected God, God had not rejected Arthur. Arthur's mother prayed fervently that her son would return to God and to the Church. God heard the prayers of a mother and in 1999, at a family wedding, Arthur was invited to go with a group to Medjugorje the following June; in the heat of the moment and in a very inebriated state, Arthur agreed with the proposition.[2]

Within a very short time, Arthur found himself in Medjugorje, bored to death, heading for the nearest bar in the village and wondering how he was going to find a way out of the place. He had no desire to join the group, those he called "professional

---

[1] The Mass is the central act of worship in the Catholic Church going back to the time of the Lord's Supper. Also: "Mass (Lat. perhaps "dismissal"): A word commonly used in the Roman Church, where the regular form of dismissal at the end of the liturgy is "Ite messa est" (Lat. "Go, the Mass is ended")" [O'Collins, G., Farrugia, E. "A Concise Dictionary of Theology", Rev. ed. (T&T Clarke, Edinburgh, 2000) 154.].

[2] McCluskey, A. "My Healing from Gambling & Alcohol in Medjugorje", 2nd ed. (Arthur McCluskey, Ireland, 2007) 10. [This book is available from Mother's Village Shop, Bijakovići bb, Medjugorje; or can be obtained by contacting Donal O'Shea, Director, "St. Joseph & The Helpers Charity", at: donal@helperscharity.com.].

6

pilgrimage holidaymakers".[3] However, the Holy Spirit was at work and whilst Arthur drowned his sorrows in the local beer whilst sitting at a table outside a bar in Medjugorje, he found himself in the company of Nicky, one of his group members.[4] When Arthur first met Nicky at Dublin airport on the journey to Medjugorje, he had pitied him, looked down on him, felt superior to him, because Nicky had a limp due to a stroke in his earlier years and, in fact, as it transpired, had been partially paralysed for forty-one years. However, God had captured Arthur in a net even though he did not realise it at that time.

Surrender

Day 1 - Humility
That first day, meeting Nicky at the bar, Arthur asked sarcastically if he had come to Medjugorje for a healing? Nicky replied with humility, touched his heart and said, "No, I have already been healed here."[5] The moment Nicky put his hand to his heart, all idea of leaving Medjugorje left Arthur and he was overwhelmed with humility.

Day 2 - Illumination
Having lived in the darkness for so long, the Holy Spirit had to illuminate Arthur's mind and heart in a powerful way to the consequences of his lifestyle. Working through the purported

---

[3] Ibid., 12-14.
[4] Ibid., 15.
[5] Ibid., 15.

visionaries Mirjana and Jakov,[6] Arthur heard for the first time in years the reality of Heaven, Purgatory and Hell and the necessity of being prepared to meet God.[7] He questioned himself; was he prepared? The answer was 'No'.[8]

Day 3 - Tears of Healing.
On day three, Arthur walked up Apparition Hill praying the Rosary and whilst he prayed, the tears started to fall.[9] He had not prayed the Rosary in thirty years, but had taken Rosary beads to Medjugorje with him, "just in case I needed them." The tears fell and realising that his life was one of sin, he could not wait to

---

[6] At the time of writing, The Catholic Church has not given authentication to the Medjugorje phenomenon and in this text the writer used the term "purported visionaries". However, as this would be burdensome throughout the book, the word "Visionaries" will be used without the word "purported".
[7]. 'Heaven': Scripture in Christianity describes it as our eternal home where God shares his divine life with us (Mathew: 25:34). 'Purgatory': (Lat. purification). State of those who die in God's friendship, but who still need their personal sins to be expiated (through the merits of Christ) and who should grow spiritually before enjoying the beatific vision. (O'Collins, G., Farrugia, E. "A Concise Dictionary of Theology", (2000) 217; 'Hell': The place or state where unrepentant sinners suffer forever – eternal punishment (Mathew 13: 36-43; 25:31-46).
[8] McCluskey, A. "My Healing from Gambling & Alcohol in Medjugorje", 2nd ed., 17.
[9] **Apparition Hill** – the local name is Podbrdo: approximately 200 metres high; **Rosary**: Meaning circle or crown of roses. These were originally beads in the shape of roses in a circle. Praying each bead is a form of meditation and repetitive prayer. In the Catholic Church this form of meditation always focuses on Mary, the Mother of Christ and on the beautiful relationship with her son Jesus (Groesschel, J. "The Rosary" (Creative Publications for The Parish, St. Louis, USA, 1995) 3.

go to Confession.[10] That night he made his first confession in over twenty years.[11]

Day 4 - The Way of the Cross.

On day four, Arthur climbed Mt. Krizevac, stopping at each station of the 'Way of the Cross', meditating on the sufferings of Jesus and how our bad life-style would appear to put a nail into Jesus on the Cross.[12] He knew that he had caused Jesus much suffering and felt deeply remorseful.[13]

---

[10] **Confession** (or Penance of Reconciliation) is the sacrament by which we, repenting and confessing our sins, are absolved of sin through the ministry of the Church by a priest [Holden, M., Pinsent, A. "Evangelium" (The Catholic Truth Society, London, 2006) 27.] The sacrament answers a deep need to confess sin, receive pardon from God and be reconciled with the community harmed by our sin.: **Sacraments** are visible signs, instituted by Christ, which reveals and communicates grace [O'Collins, G., Farrugia, E. "A Concise Dictionary of Theology", Rev. ed. (T&T Clarke, Edinburgh, 2000) 231].

[11]McCluskey, A. "My Healing from Gambling & Alcohol in Medjugorje", 2nd ed. (2007) 18-30.

[12] **Mount Krizevac**, known as 'Cross-Mountain': approximately 500 metres high. Also called Cross-Mountain due to the 33ft. Cross built on the top; **Stations of the Cross**: The 'Way of the Cross' which Jesus walked to Golgotha to be crucified. The devotion is represented by plaques depicting the journey of Christ from condemnation to death: 1) Jesus is condemned to die; 2) Jesus carries His Cross, 3) Jesus falls the first time, 4) Jesus meets his mother, 5) Simon helps Jesus carry His cross, 6) Veronica wipes Jesus' face, 7) Jesus falls for the 2nd time, 8) Jesus meets the women of Jerusalem, 9) Jesus falls the 3rd time, 10) Jesus is stripped of his clothing, 11) Jesus is nailed to the cross, 12) Jesus dies on the cross, 13) Jesus is taken down from the cross, 14) Jesus is laid in the tomb (Barry, W. "The Stations of the Cross by St. Francis of Assisi" (Catholic Book Publishing Co., New York, 1968).

[13] McCluskey, A. "My Healing from Gambling & Alcohol in Medjugorje", 2nd ed. (2007) 31.

Day 5 –Our Lady's Messages[14].

On day five, Arthur listened with hope in his heart to Vicka, one of the Visionaries, bringing Our Lady's message of joy, peace and happiness and Arthur felt a great surge of hope, joy and longing for life.[15]

Day 6 – Surrender

On day six, Arthur climbed back up to the top of Mt. Krizevac, placed his hand on the base of the cross and surrendered, saying, **"Jesus, I am Yours forever."**[16]

A New Goal

Arthur had a new goal.   No longer was his goal to make money for himself; his new goal was to help the people of Bosnia and Herzegovina rebuild their lives after the 1992-1995 Bosnian war. Arthur turned his focus away from gambling and moved back to Ireland where he worked for four years with 'Rebuild for Bosnia', provided housing for over seventy families. Eventually his humanitarian work led him and a team of directors to start a new charity, "St Joseph & The Helpers" so that they could raise money and spread awareness of the great need for help in Bosnia and Herzegovina.[17]   Tirelessly Arthur responded to invitations to give talks throughout Ireland, Scotland, and England as well as to groups in Medjugorje, telling them of his freedom from gambling

---

[14] "Our Lady" is a name of endearment used by Catholics and given to Mary, the mother of Jesus Christ.
[15] McCluskey, A. "My Healing from Gambling & Alcohol in Medjugorje", 2nd ed. (2007) 32.
[16] Ibid. 33-34.
[17] Ibid. 56-59.

and of the work of the new charity, established in Ireland on May 19th and in the UK on 24th November 2004.

Within a short time the charity's first project emerged, that of building the Kindergarten School in Kiseljak, soon to be followed by many new projects which continue to this day.

The Projects:

Over €3,000,000 has been raised for the following projects;

- **Kindergarten School, Kiseljak (2004):** This first project was the building of a Franciscan Kindergarten School for 150 children in Kiseljak, near Sarajevo. The charity has an ongoing commitment to cover all heating, lighting and maintenance costs each year at the Kindergarten School. Money was also raised for a mini-bus, 90 new cots and beds purchased in 2011 and new storage closets in 2012.

- **Visoko:** The Franciscan Secondary School in Visoko, near Sarajevo. In addition to the charity's contribution to support this project, funds were sourced from a Company Trust in Dusseldorf by one of the directors.

- **Mother's Village,** Bijakovici, near Medjugorje: for orphans and children whose parents are so damaged they cannot cater for the needs of young people and for the rehabilitation of young men suffering from addictions. The charity provided the funds to build St Joseph's Hall and supports the upkeep of the children.

- **Sr. Kornelijie and her Order, the Missionary Sisters of the Family Wound,** run the Grandparents Home at Vionica and also the John Paul II Orphanages at Citluk and Vionica. St Joseph & The Helpers have supported Sr Kornelijie in her work.

  - o **Grandparents Home in Vionica.** Providing funds to build the Home. The shell of the building was up, but funds were exhausted. St Joseph & The Helpers provided €90,000 to complete the building including €40,000 for a lift.

  - o **John Paul II Orphanage, Citluk:** Provision of financial help.

  - o **John Paul II Orphanage, Vionica:** Provision of financial help. In 2012 the charity paid €10,500 for maintenance work.

- **Miracles Centre for Prosthetic Care, near Potoci, Mostar.** The charity provides ongoing support for the provision of prosthetic limbs to very grateful amputees. For many years the charity funded seaside holidays for between 40 and 60 orphans.

- **Dezevice:** Refurbishment of the parish house and church, as well as financial support for the Visitors' Centre (2012).

- **Zenica:** St Joseph Parish: Parish House and Convent refurbishment.

- **Prozor Rama - Prozor parish:** Funding renovation of the parish house.

- **Franciscan Kindergarten, Bijelo Polje, near Mostar.** Providing equipment, furnishing the sleeping areas, two classrooms and kitchen. The charity is now helping to equip and develop the playground. A kind pilgrim who travelled with St Joseph & The Helpers group in 2012, donated funds for some playground equipment and landscaping.

- **St Luke's Home Care: Founder, Jane Dowd.** Assisting Jane Dowd by funding one of her four nurses who care for the sick, elderly and disabled in their homes in over 50 villages around Medjugorje.

- **D...... Family:** Through a single donation to the charity, a house was built for the family.

- **Refugee families:** Built a house for a refugee family. In 2012, a kind donor to the charity bought an apartment for a refugee family who were about to be evicted. In 2013, a house was totally insulated for a refugee family in Hodovo. Without insulation, the house had been like an oven in summer and a fridge in winter.

- **Families and Individuals in dire need of help:** monthly financial aid and at Christmas a donation is shared amongst families by Sr Jelenka.

- **Computers:** Providing computers for a convent hostel in Mostar and educational sponsorship for some of the young female students who live there.

In June 2011, Arthur and two UK directors visited two projects which had requested funding: The Youth Centre in Sarajevo and the Pastoral Centre and Public Kitchen at Dobrinja which needed a lot of money to complete. Arthur wanted to help both projects and was excited about finding sponsorship for free meals at the Public Kitchen in due course. Sadly, he passed away in August 2011 before the projects were realised.

- **Pastoral Centre and Public Kitchen in Sarajevo.** Run by Father Pero Karajica and feeding 300 people daily. The shell of the building was up and they had run out of funds. The charity raised funds to complete the centre and kitchen.

- **Youth Centre, Sarajevo.** To honour Arthur's wish to help the project, financial provision to help the youth centre was donated in 2012.

- **Scholarships:** Fifteen scholarships for students to attend Sarajevo University were funded by a donation from Irvine Marian Conference held in October 2011. The charity currently provides ongoing support for fees, books, living costs and transport for three young women to college and university. They would very much like to set up scholarships for young students at Mother's Village.

Temptation

However, it was not always easy for Arthur. For three years after his surrender, Arthur still had a compulsion to gamble. He did not admit himself to a clinic for treatment, or seek psychological or psychiatric help. Arthur could not change his past. He did not need to dwell on it. Fr Svet helped him to understand that his years as an addict were turned to prayer. God had forgiven him and that was all that mattered. He lived his life, focusing on his new goal, his new life, and his new mission.

Arthur's treatment was both simple and powerful: he focused on his new goal and he used Our Lady's spiritual weapons to achieve that goal.

1. **New goal** – that of helping the people of Bosnia and Herzegovina.

2. **Our Lady's Weapons:**

- **Prayer with the Heart:**
  Arthur started his day with prayer for two hours. During the day he prayed many Rosaries.

- **Eucharist**
  Arthur went to Mass daily and received Holy Communion.

- **Holy Bible**
  He replaced his old ways of reading gambling newspapers with reading the Scriptures, reading the Bible daily, being encouraged by God's Word.

- **Fasting**
  For some years after his conversion, Arthur fasted on bread and water on Wednesday and Friday and the special Feast Days of the Church, praying for the intentions of many, but especially for the people of Bosnia and Herzegovina. However, ill health intervened and his doctor advised him to be less harsh on himself.

- **Monthly confession:**
Arthur was not perfect; he knew he needed to keep close to God. He refused to allow his transgressions to ruin his life. He turned to God in repentance, time, after time, after time.

Liberation

Arthur focused on the work of St Joseph & The Helpers Charity in Bosnia and Herzegovina and was liberated. He never gambled again. He replaced arrogance with humility, self-indulgence with compassion. He dedicated the rest of his life to serving others. Arthur remained free of his addiction permanently.

On August 13, 2011, Arthur suffered a heart attack and died suddenly. His work on earth was finished, but his work continues on through the charity he founded, St Joseph & The Helpers.

The Work of His Hands......

Arthur worked closely with his fellow directors to ensure that the work of the charity remained focused. However, throughout his time in Bosnia and Herzegovina, Arthur depended on two of his closest friends for moral support and encouragement.

The first is Vesna Radišić, owner of 'Pansion St. Michael' in Medjugorje. Without her local knowledge, her love of the Franciscan Priests and Sisters, many of the projects would have gone unheeded. Vesna quietly and firmly pointed Arthur in the direction of those who were most in need. Arthur trusted Vesna totally, and respected her commitment to God and her compassion for her fellow man. Arthur regarded Vesna as one of his closest friends. He spoke of her with deep affection, praise and admiration.

The second is Donal O'Shea, one of the first Directors of the Charity. Time and time again Arthur would relate how much he depended on Donal; how he could not be without him and how much he respected and trusted his judgement and his integrity. Arthur and Donal worked together closely and effectively. They were a team. Arthur regarded Donal as one of his closest and trusted friends and confidants.

The following chapters relate the story of God's amazing work through Arthur McCluskey, who gave his life to Jesus, turned away from gambling forever and focused on the needs of the people of Bosnia and Herzegovina. Each chapter has a story to tell from the perspective of the people in Bosnia and Herzegovina. Each chapter reveals the power of the Holy Spirit working through St Joseph & The Helpers with the purpose of bringing humanitarian aid to a people Arthur grew to love and for whom he worked tirelessly. This is a story of the fruits of his labour, the story of love, freedom and hope.

Chapter I

The Work of the Franciscan Sisters at Kiseljak and Bijelo Polje

1. Kiseljak

The Bosnian war had wreaked havoc on the lives of the Franciscan Sisters of Christ the King, but never more so than in Kiseljak, a small town in Bosnia close to Sarajevo, where there were great losses in the community; where many men and women were killed. Many lost their families, their homes, everything that had been permanent and familiar and where eventually, in despair, many moved away from the region. Very few returned and those who did were faced with a collapsed social system where unemployment in Kiseljak reached 60%-90% after the war. Each day a steady stream of men and women trod the path of desperation and hope to seek work, often without success, leaving their children to fend for themselves during the day. There were few people left to care for the children: grandparent, aunts and uncles were lost to them, dead or missing or so traumatised that normality was a goal too difficult to achieve. The Sisters knew that without their intervention, without their help, the generation would be lost to the confusion and heartlessness of the world around them. They knew how important it was, not only to give the children a loving safe haven during the day, but to provide a place where they could start re-building a shattered community through the tool of education.

Whilst acknowledging that the provision of a nursery school was the answer for a stable future, the Sisters conceded that it would take a miracle to provide the financial assistance required to build such an ambitious project. However, miracles were the norm for Sr Jelenka, Head of the Province, for she had witnessed the protection, the care and the providence of God, time and time again during the war; and so the Sisters prayed. With humility and determination, in their little Chapel in the convent, they laid the "kindergarten plan" before God and sought His guidance, His help, His inspiration.

Slowly, the Lord guided them to re-build the Chapel which had been closed by the communists in 1960. Fortunately, the Croatian government wished to protect the Chapel since it was part of a monument important to Bosnia and Herzegovina, so they provided the money to enable the Sisters to claim back and restore their Chapel. Once more the people had a place to worship and so they gathered together, the community and the Sisters, and prayed that the Lord would provide the money for the much needed kindergarten. With prayer came action and the Sisters wrote to a variety of organisations and one wrote back asking them if they had one third of the amount required for the project and if they did, they would provide the rest. No, they did not have any money and they hoped that God would help, Sr Jelenka responded. They also hoped that the local county office would assist them with finance since they had given the Sisters the necessary permission to build the kindergarten. Limited help came from those avenues, but not enough for the project to come to fruition. Eventually, from various other sources came enthusiastic offers of help, promising to give donations to the Sisters for this worthwhile project.

Sr Jelenka believed from the very beginning that building the kindergarten was the will of God but at one time she began to doubt that she had understood God's will, for the amount of money that trickled to her doorstop was relatively small, 5,000 or 10,000 Euros, in relation to the amount required for this huge project. She began to doubt that the project would ever be completed with such small amounts of money.   In humility, she turned back to God relating to Him that if she had not understood Him and that this was not His will, then she and the Sisters would walk away; but, if it were His will, would He please provide the means to fund the project.   The Sisters waited; they prayed and they waited and God heard the gentle prayers of His loving, faithful daughters.

In 2004 Maura McGrath, an Irish lady, happened to be staying at the warm and welcoming 'Pansion St. Michael' in Medjugorje belonging to Vesna & Miran Radišić. Maura had introduced Arthur McCluskey to Vesna several years previously and Arthur and Vesna had become good friends. Now Vesna is a very prayerful lady who loves God with all her heart and devotes herself to helping all those who cross her path.   She loves the gentle Franciscan Sisters and one in particular, Sr Dominika, who at that time was based at the kindergarten in Medjugorje and had become a frequent visitor to Vesna's house.

Vesna had suggested to the Sisters that perhaps Maura might know of someone in Ireland who would be able to help them with the finance to build a new kindergarten in Kiseljak.   Sr Dominika relayed this to Sr Jelenka and, prompted by the Holy Spirit and armed with determination and the recognition of a window of opportunity, Sr Jelenka wrote a letter to accompany the kindergarten plans and instructed Sr Dominika to dispatch them to the appropriate person who could help, who happened to be Maura.   Maura had no idea who to ask for help but accepted the plans and the accompanying letter and on her return to Ireland, sought out the help of her brother Donal O'Shea, who had just become one of the Directors of Arthur McCluskey's newly founded "St Joseph & The Helpers" charity. Donal opened the carefully written letter and read:

" September, 2004.

Dear Sir or Madam,

I am writing to you on behalf of Franciscan School Sisters of Christ the King of the Holy Family Province, which I represent as Head Principal of the province.   The province has a headquarter in Mostar, Herzegovina, but the Sisters act in different places in the home country and abroad, even on other continents.   But the main field of work of this province is situated on the area of Bosnia and Herzegovina which heals the wounds it received in the recent war.

Basic charisma of the Franciscan school Sister's community is guiding of young people.   Regarding this mission and needs of this moment, the Holy Family Province tries to be involved with people's lives.   So we decided in Kiseljak, little town in Bosnia, which suffers greats losses in this war, both in people and in material destructions, to help with our contribution to educate the young people.

Since the town lacks facility of a nursery school it has become the prime objective of the local church and the community.   To this end we desperately need financial assistance and in the name of the Holy Family school Sister's province I ask your help.
Enclosed is a copy of the project.   The project has many purposes: primary to work with children in the nursery school, but we would also like to

21

*organize spiritual renewals, seminars for young
people and married couples.*

*Hopefully you will support our work and help us to
fulfil our idea. In anticipation we thank you from
our heart. As benefactors you will certainly be
involved in everyday prayers of our sisters.*

Yours faithfully,

**Franciscan Sschool Sisters of the Holy Family
Province**

**S. Jelenka Puljić
Head Principal of the Province"**

Donal discussed the letter and plans with Arthur and they agreed to
meet Sr Dominika in October 2004 in Medgugorje. "How much will
it cost, Sister?" enquired Arthur. "Just one moment," replied Sr
Dominika and much to Arthur's surprise, she reached into her pocket,
retrieved a mobile phone and made a call to Sr Jelenka. "He never
quite recovered from the realisation that nuns also carry mobile
phones," chuckles Donal. "He had an entirely different perception of
them. He often laughed about that moment."

Perhaps that was the moment that clinched the deal, or perhaps it was
Sr Dominika's beautiful, endearing smile, or maybe it was just the
Holy Spirit at work, for the deal was done.
Arthur returned to Ireland and travelled to every crevice of the land
telling people of this little place in Bosnia called Kiseljak, where
unemployment ran on average at 80%, where both parents were out

looking for work and the children were without adequate supervision; he wanted help for these children. God heard Arthur's call and He touched the hearts of the warm hearted people of Ireland, those who had the means to give to those who had not, and money came pouring into St Joseph & The Helpers, all the money required for the project, some €585,000.

Sr Jelenka reflects that when she met Arthur at a later time, she had the impression that he was holding back. "He speaks a little, but...she had hope. He was a serious man but had a sense of humour. They were joking that soon they would be running an Alcoholic Anonymous meeting at the convent." Sr Jelenka prayed every day for the project and for the benefactors and she smiles when she recalls that when Cardinal Vinko Puljic came to visit in 2005 to see how the project was going, he said that the Sisters should be running the country.

Sr Jelenka was filled with gratitude and she thanked God for this new and wonderful source of help. Her relentlessness to help her people, to do the will of God, was coming to fruition, but it was also raising incredulity amongst the other churches in her neighbourhood, a powerful witness to trust in God always. "Who is giving you money?" they asked. "It is God's providence" she would smile quietly. The people of Ireland and the United Kingdom (UK) had responded with amazing generosity and love; they reached out across the borders, one mother to another mother, one husband to another husband, one community to another, sharing the pain, sharing the despair, but knowing that there is always hope; and because they cared, they gave and they gave unconditionally.

The Kindergarten was built in two stages. The two storey building was put up and the upper part sealed off while the school was developed on the ground floor. It was the charity's intention to fund only the school but the directors loved the project so much that they continued to appeal for funds and completed the convent and meeting rooms on the upper floor. In October 2007, the Kindergarten was officially opened and the first Mass was said in the Convent Chapel by Cardinal Vinko Puljic. Other Franciscan priests concelebrated including Fr Mijo Dzolan, The Franciscan Provincial at that time. Sr Jelenka quietly stood up to the microphone and with a mixture of pride, happiness, shyness and humility she spoke:

"Your Excellency the Cardinal, dear Priests, dear Friends, Benefactors of St Joseph & The Helpers society, dear Sisters,

With a sincere and joyful heart that I greet all of you, especially our dear Cardinal. I welcome all of you here on behalf of St Joseph & The Helpers, Mr. Arthur McCluskey, and the directors representing the other branches.

Our gathering this evening is a sign of our gratitude, thanksgiving and joy. We are grateful to God for His divine providence in sending us these dear people with kind and generous hearts who helped to make the building of this facility a reality. Looking back to my words when we first opened, I said that if anything concrete was a result of all the prayers, it was the realisation of this project and the purpose for it; that is to take care of and raise the children.

Four years ago, when it was still questionable whether or not the Sisters would stay in this area, the suggestion came forward to remodel the old chapel. In Archive – the file of this Parish was written that back in the 19th century it was a chapel; it actually served as the main church. During the days of Communism it served as a hidden chapel for those who wanted to receive the sacraments, but weren't allowed to. After those days the chapel served as a storage area. During the remodelling process a historically significant monument was discovered. After the remodelling, Eminence, Cardinal, you have blessed the Chapel and accepted our recommendation to dedicate it to 'Our Lady of Angels' where we would hold daily and perpetual adoration with the people. A few months after the chapel was dedicated, the idea was formed to build the pre-school, which was so much needed for this area. The realisation of this idea happened so quickly as if it took on a life of its own. We blessed the foundation and began building, believe it or not, without money in hand. Many promised donations, but most of those remained just promises. Despite the other hardships we encountered, for which I do not want to elaborate, I prayed, dear God, give us a sign if it is not your will for this pre-school to be built we will stop. I won't be embarrassed to stop with the construction.

The sign we received was a group of Medjugorje pilgrims, whose leader was Mr Arthur McCluskey, who promised to help in building the pre-school. I believe the prayers in this little porcinucula – Chapel of 'Our Lady of Angels', Sisters' prayers were answered. The project moved so quickly even you, dear bishop, had something to say about it. After a soccer game in the autumn that you attended, you came to visit our community and commented jokingly to the provincial, Fr. Mijo, about how quickly the building was moving forward and that the Sisters should work in economics. My response was that it was not a thing of economics, but rather a thing of the knees.

My dear friends, I am not certain whether or not you feel the effects of our constant prayers, but I feel and believe that you do. We, the Sisters, pray for you daily: May Lord Jesus Christ bless you and your families. May your beloved Country of Ireland be always blessed and covered with Motherly love of Queen of Peace and protection of Her Spouse, St Joseph. [1]

The times we live in are constantly battling and suggesting the best way to raise children and we want to join in this battle as well by instilling in them the spirit of Christian values. They will also be grateful knowing that you helped them become educated and how to be the carriers of peace and to create a better world. They will know that a part of the Irish spirit was built into this facility and that it is the same spirit which unites us.

Your eminence, thank you for celebrating holy Eucharist for us gathered and especially for our friends with generous hearts and gentle hands. May the dear Lord refresh us so that we may continue to promote goodness, peace and joy."

Sr. Jelenka Puljic, provinciale".

Donal reflects that shortly after the charity made a decision in 2004 to help, there was a Tsunami in the Far East and all the money in Ireland was being collected for the Tsunami. Arthur expressed his concerns to Sr Jelenka who responded that there could be another Tsunami in six months time, in other words, 'trust in God, go out there and raise the funds'.

---

[1] Author's footnote: At that time, the majority of benefactors were from Ireland.

Entering the little iron gate and following the rows of colourful flowers, the path leads to the front steps of the kindergarten. The plaque proudly displays a "St Joseph & The Helpers Charity" inscription, acknowledging that without them, there would be no kindergarten. The polished door bell invites the visitor to summon the staff inside and in response to the persistent ring, a smiling Sister throws open the doors and invites the visitor in. The rainbow colours dance around the polished floors reflecting the flowers, the paintings, the toys, the little tables and chairs, the laughter of the children.

Small rows of tables are neatly prepared for the mid-day meal. Little hands fold gently, eyes close and the thanksgiving prayers flutter quietly and soar to Heaven. The children sit down and like all children the world over, some eat hastily, some toss the food around in their plate and some forget to eat because they are too busy chatting; but they are eating. Over 100 children under the age of six years attend the school, some of them with special needs. They can be assured that each day during the week, there will be a meal, beautifully prepared by the Sisters, to ensure that they are nourished, that they will grow in health, in confidence, in trust of one another. For this is the future of Bosnia and Herzegovina; it is Christian, Serb and Muslim children eating together, laughing together, praying together and growing with each other in love. There are no favourites in God's world, for each child is created in His image.[2] This is not, therefore, just a kindergarten, a class for schoolchildren, a place to play and be cared for during the day, it is part of the foundation for peace, security and harmony in Bosnia and Herzegovina in the years ahead.

---

[2] Genesis 1:27. "God created man in the image of himself, in the image of God he created him, male and female he created them." [The New Jerusalem Bible: Study Edition .(Darton, Longman & Todd, London, 1994)]

In 2006, Sr Jelenka wrote a letter of appreciation to all the Helpers:

"Greetings and God's blessings from Kiseljak, a small town in Bosnia that is slowly recovering from the war!

Grateful to God and His providence and to you, dear friends, Kiseljak now has a place for our children. Namely, so far Kiseljak did not have any kindergarten facility or day care or any place for our little ones. That is why this institution is so well received by the parents, teachers, church groups, social and political institutions. We are planning to make room for 150 children. So far, we accommodate 60 children in two groups. We are witnessing the children's joy and smiles, the parents' happiness and pride every day. Our Sisters are so grateful to God and to all our benefactors who built and equipped the facility. The interest for continuing to furnish the remaining part of the facility is great and we look with confidence to divine providence which will once again realise itself through the members of St Joseph & The Helpers.

With this, an additional 100 children, that is families, could be assisted in raising children in Christian and human morality as well as employing ten additional workers.[3] There is a great number of unemployed and in this manner we can assist in reducing that number, even though it may be a minimal amount.

It is understood that the facility is open to all children of all ethnic groups. As we Franciscan school sisters lead the

---

[3] Author's note: All religions are respected at the kindergarten and children are encouraged to pray accordingly.

facility, it is evident that the spiritual dimension is incorporated in the program. Every day we have benediction services and all of those who assist us are included in our prayers. There is also a part of the facility which is named after your protector, St Joseph the Helper, as a sign of gratitude for your gift. We are grateful for your readiness and for your generosity to help us to finish what still remains so that we can bring smiles to more children and to their homes.

Through the intercession of the Queen of Peace and St Joseph, may the good Lord keep you and protect you.

On behalf of the Franciscan School Sisters,

Sr. Jelenka Puljic, Mother Provincial.[4]

The work is full-time. Upstairs above the kindergarten, the Sisters settle into their new convent. The old one is situated a short walk away, next to the little Chapel on the hill, but the new one built above the kindergarten means that there is always someone in the building, always someone to take care of any child who may need help. The table is set and the Sisters sit down to their evening meal. The day has been busy, prayers in the early hours imploring God for his Wisdom during the day. The children arrive very early, sometimes at 6 a m, most at 7 a m, but the Sisters are ready and the activity of the day leaves them tired but very happy. During the day the children snuggle into their little cots to regenerate their energy levels for play

---

[4] Letter of Appreciation from Mother Provincial, Bosnia and Herzegovina, 2006.

in the afternoon, but the Sisters catch up with other chores at this time, so they never have time to rest.[5]

The evening meal is respite from the busy day. The food arrives; it is simple, but cooked beautifully – nutritious fish, potatoes, green beans and the most delicious of carrot cakes, all washed down by the wine from Sr Anna's uncle's vineyard. One Sister is fasting; one always makes the sacrifice for the community as an offering to God in thanksgiving for all that has been provided.

At any time the door bell may ring, for the Sisters are constantly ready to help their neighbours. When the people have problems, they come to speak to Sr Jelenka, trusting in her quiet, understanding, non-judgemental caring ways and confidentiality. There are many broken people; many hurt and bewildered families struggling to cope with poverty, pain and loss of hope.

One day the convent bell rang and when Sr Jelenka responded, a distressed, gentle woman stood nervously and requested an interview with her. Sr Jelenka opened the door and invited her in and with dignity, this gentle woman broke down as she related her concerns in a desperate plea for help.

Vesna D. and her husband have two children.[6] At one time she had lived in her father's house, but they could not live with her father because her sister lived there and there was not enough room; furthermore, the house was in equally bad condition to her own. Her father had given her this house to live in but it was in a dilapidated condition, cold, leaking, in great disrepair, with an outside toilet and

---

[5] In 2011, St Joseph & The Helpers paid €5,400 to provide 90 new beds and cots for the sleeping area.

[6] Surname withheld for reasons of confidentiality. ('Vesna' – not to be confused with Vesna Radišić, Arthur's friend in Medjugorje.)

outside cooking facilities. Vesna had felt very alone. Her husband worked night shift and she could not sleep; her mind in a turmoil and full of painful images of her brothers' deaths. The toilet was outside the house and she and the children were afraid to go out at night. Her husband was considering selling one of his kidneys so that they would have some money to start building a house. Sr Jelenka asked her why she did not manage to receive a donation after the war because the government were giving donations to refugees. Vesna replied that she had been asked by one corrupt official to give some money to the authorities so that she could acquire the donation, money that she did not have. so she never received one euro of help. Unfortunately Vesna's situation was never brought to the attention of the honest authorities representing the government, who would have ensured that she received government help. The meeting was intense but Sr Jelenka arranged to go and visit Vesna in her house. In July 2011, Sister appealed to the wider community for help for the family and wrote:

"Dear Friends,

I began my way to Kresevski Kamenik. I drove to the end of the village, which also was the end of the asphalt road. The road is narrow and I had to drive carefully to pass by cars coming from the other side. The road was rough and I had to leave my car behind and walk the rest. The family's son met me on the road and escorted me down the narrow road leading to their house. I had to keep looking away from the beauty of the nature surrounding their house to be able to look at the reality of what was the interior and exterior of their house. The hidden smiles and cheeriness of their mother Vesna were encouraging, as if they were saying, "we're healthy, we're together, and we believe and hope in God's providence".

Vesna was born in a small village.[7] *Her parents had seven children. Their house was in equally bad shape interior and exterior. Her mother suffered from rheumatoid arthritis for 23 years. For the last seven years of her life, she was completely immobile. One of Vesna's brothers drowned at the age of seven years. Three of Vesna's brothers were soldiers in the war from 1992-1995. Unfortunately, the effects of war were too great on these men and all three of them suffered psychologically - post traumatic stress disorder.*

Her younger brother, who was 23 years old, hanged himself in the barn near their home in 1998. Her older brother, aged 37, also hanged himself in 2010.[8]

Vesna was married in 1999 to her husband Ivo who was a refugee from another village. He is a hard worker who had a stable job up until three years ago. He was a cement worker. As they were unable to find better housing, and would have to pay for something better, they decided to live in the house which I have described above. They have no indoor plumbing. They have two children, a son who is ten years old and completing 4th grade and also a good student, as well as a daughter who is seven years old and completing 1st grade. The daughter was born with a defect of her right arm which means she cannot lift it over her shoulder. This is causing her spine to be unaligned. Twice a year she goes to Kiseljak, 15 km. away, for physical therapy and other therapy in Fojnic, located 30 km away. Since their house is located in an isolated area, the nearest town is 15 minutes

---

[7] For the purpose of confidentiality the author has edited part of this letter by removing surnames.

[8] Vesna's son, witnessed the death scene of his uncle.

away on foot. During the winter with back-packs on their shoulders, the children must walk through the forest for ten minutes where they wait for a bus to take them to school. They bring a change of socks and boots to change out of their snow-filled boots. It is this way each day and the Bosnian winters are extremely cold and snowy.

Vesna's husband even considered donating a kidney for money in order to begin building a house. His wife was able to talk him out of this, since he would not be able to work the hard labour that he is used to on one kidney.

Vesna's father is prepared to give them land on which to build their house.

I don't know what else I could write, except that when I returned from their house I went to the Chapel and prayed the sorrowful mysteries of the rosary for this family and for all those who will help them. I believe that God will send them help. I heard an interior voice that I should not be afraid to send this letter – an appeal for help, since there are so many good people who will be happy to help this family to build a new home for their family, to help the terrible situation of this family. This will solidify within them the presence of God's providence which touches others to remember those in need. With this faith and hope I send this letter and place all of you in this project in God's providence."[9]

Sr. Jelenka Puljic, Mother Provincial

---

[9] Letter from Sr Jelenka received by St Joseph & The Helpers Charity in August 2011.

In November 2011, in a little hamlet, just off the beaten track, a little while stone built house gleams in the sunshine. The little family proudly open the door and welcome their visitors to their almost finished house. The bathroom is the star attraction of the tour boasting fresh looking blue and cream tiles, a new shower, a new basin and both a toilet and a bidet. This is part of their dream, that and the little kitchen fitted snugly next to the living-room, a gift from Nikodil the builder from Kiseljak, as were the windows. The corridor branches into the children's bedroom, one room for one boy and one girl to share, perhaps not ideal in the modern context, but the children have their very own bedroom, their very own space and they no longer have to share that space with their mother and father. Nor do mother and father have to share their treasured privacy with the children, for at the other end of the corridor opposite the bathroom, Vesna and her husband have their very own bedroom. Opposite their bedroom, next to the bathroom, a stone staircase invites the family to climb to the next floor where the attic, roof raised and dormer windows inserted, an innovative idea coming to fruition also by the generosity of Nikodil, lies ready for the final conversion to include two more rooms. That is for the future, for that means finding another €5,000. Right at this moment, the family are grateful for the gift of their new home which has been funded through St Joseph & The Helpers by one donor, one person with a beautiful and generous heart, who reached out to a family, strangers in a far away land and donated €32,000 to change their lives forever.

The family have very little furniture and much of it is worn and unusable, but unexpectedly the neighbouring community banded together and provided various items to furnish their home. Two days before Christmas 2011, they moved into their new house and with gratitude and love they sent the following letter to those who had made it possible to achieve their dream:

"Dear Friends,

*The day we finished our house was the most
fantastic and the happiest day of our lives. This
couldn't be possible without your help.*

*My family can't thank you enough for all you
have done for us. You are in our prayers.*

Sincerely,

Sometime later, in January 2012, €1,000 was donated to the charity
to provide specialist therapy for the treatment of the little daughter's
shoulder.   This family is just one family in the mosaic of the Sisters'
lives. There are many families in similar situations and many families
who still suffer terrible psychological problems as a result of the
Bosnian war.   Already Sr Jelenka has spent a great deal of time
counselling depressed persons; families whose husbands are
alcoholics and young people who are failing in school due to the
fragmented fabric of the family and society.   She sees results,
positive results, encouraging her to continue with the work God has
entrusted into her care.

 Sr Jelenka looks to the future when she can convert the old convent
and use it as a counselling centre for those families who suffer from
post-war syndrome, for treatment of addicts in Kiseljak and where
they can hold spiritual retreats.   There are many families and young
people who have been destroyed by addictions, unwanted
pregnancies and violence.   They will fix the floors and put in new
windows and renovate the convent.   They will plant window boxes
and flowers in the garden and provide a peaceful venue for broken
hearts and broken lives.

Sr Jelenka also plans to organise 'Alcoholic Anonymous' (AA) meetings in Kiseljak as well as other villages and towns within 50 to 100 kilometres to fight against alcohol problems.   In addition, the Sisters consider it a priority to offer accommodation to young pregnant girls and women who experience violence in their families. They know that all of this will take time and patience, but the Sisters have great hopes for the future and for the healing of their nation.

One hope is for more children in the kindergarten and another that God will continue to help.   They are grateful for the gift of the Volkswagen Minibus for the children with special needs, provided by St Joseph & The Helpers. The Sisters are totally dependent on the generosity of others to keep the kindergarten open.   Donal reminds Sr Jelenka that St Joseph & The Helpers have pledged over €20,000 per year for the maintenance, heating and lighting costs of the kindergarten.   She smiles, reassured that in spite of Arthur's death, the work will continue.

2.   Kindergarten at Bijelo Polje

Further south, near to Mostar, in Bijelo Polje (white fields), Sr Dominika settles in to her new room having moved from Kiseljak to take over the running of the new kindergarten adjoining the Sisters' newly built convent.   The Convent's journey has been tumultuous and although the present day convent nestles majestically at the foot of the hills, it had humble beginnings.

According to their 'Information Leaflet', in 1899 Bishop Buconjić of Mostar bequeathed his land to the Sisters in order to provide a subsidiary of the orphanage in Mostar.[10] By 1913, there was a public primary school for both the orphanage and the local children but due to the troubles caused by World War I, there was great poverty for many years. Unfortunately, in 1921 the house in Bijelo Polje burnt down but was then rebuilt. When nationalisation took eleven houses from the Sisters in 1949, all the Sisters who had not left the community or who had not been imprisoned by the Communist authorities, came to Bijelo Polje. In 1954, the novitiate was renewed and the house in Bijelo Polje became the Provincial House as well as the house of formation.

In the summer of 1991, the Provincial Administration moved back to the newly equipped house in Mostar. The war from 1992-1995, which was to devastate many lives, eventually came to the front door of the Sisters in Bijelo Polje. However, before the fighting became intense, the majority of the Sisters were evacuated from Bijelo Polje to Baška Voda and other places and although they longed to return, many never saw Bijelo Polje again. On April 27th 1992, the convent was bombarded for the first time; no one was killed but the Sisters left the convent under shellfire. The Sisters continued to live in the convent from time to time until it was set on fire by long-range shells. On May 17th, the last of the Sisters left, withdrawing with The Croatian Defence Council Soldiers.[11]

However, eventually the convent was completely demolished by mortar fire from Mostar during the conflict and everything of value removed. Today, there is only a ruin, yet it emanates an inexplicable strength, a longevity, as if it were sleeping; like the Phoenix waiting to come to life. Indeed many pray that one day God will provide the

---

[10] "Školske sestre franjevke Krista Kralja (School Franciscan Sisters of Christ the King) Bijelo Polje [Nakladnik, Provincijalat Školskih Sestra Franjevaka Provincije S.V. Obitelji, Zagrebačka 9, Mostar].
[11] Ibid.

necessary funding so that it will be re-built as a Catholic Secondary School, a luminous sign of Christ's eternal love radiating to all people in the neighbourhood regardless of ethnicity or religion and open to all, just as the little kindergarten which now sits next to the bombed out convent, is open to all children of all religions.

The little kindergarten at Bijelo Polje gleams with newness. It is the ending of the day and most of the children have gone home to their parents, but Sr John Paul and a junior Sister still have four children to care for in the afternoon. They sit chatting round a little table with chopped up apples, oranges and bananas to pick from; a snack, an afternoon treat before the ending of the day. The four little ones are tired; playing on the swings and the balancing pole in the playground is exhausting work. Once there was a forest next to the kindergarten, but now there is only grass and wild flowers. At one time the flowers were used to make soap and hand-cream; beautiful little flowers with special herbal properties for healing the skin. The little kitten wraps his body round the Sisters' long dresses. He is a stray, like the many strays in the neighbourhood, but like the 1,300 children now in kindergartens throughout Bosnia and Herzegovina, he has found refuge amongst the Sisters.

The children arrive in the morning and some start the day with a hearty breakfast laid out carefully by the Sisters. Their day is adventurous; full of things to do, to see, to make, to learn both inside and outside the kindergarten and by lunch-time the children are hungry and ready for the nourishment which will fuel their little bodies, followed by a welcome afternoon nap.

The Sisters are innovative and their talents inexhaustible as they utilise the scarce resources to provide artistic treasures that will stimulate the minds and hands of their young protégés. A tearful child is cradled tenderly in their arms; a cut finger is patched up with great solemnity and a sleepy child is allowed the luxury of 'catching up' with those lost hours, perhaps deprived in a tumultuous home. Their dedication is overshadowed by their obvious joy in caring for the children and seeds are planted firmly and with purpose to ensure a strong generation of faith for the future.

In May 2011, St Joseph & The Helpers were approached by the Sisters asking for help with furnishing and equipping the newly built kindergarten at Bijelo Polje. Arthur understood that Sr Dominika would move from Kiseljak to set up the new school. In June 2011, he and two UK Directors visited Bijelo Polje. Arthur asked Sr Marija to obtain quotes for the classroom and sleeping areas as soon as possible as he recognised the urgency if the Kindergarten was to open in September. "What about the kitchen?" asked Sr. Marija. Arthur grinned at his two companions and replied, "Well, get two separate quotes and we'll see!" Shortly afterwards the directors were happy to contribute the necessary funds required for furniture for two classrooms and sleeping areas, as well as a brand new kitchen. Even at the cost of €30,255, the charity considered the money well-spent, as the Kindergarten had over thirty applications for places prior to its opening in September 2011. In Bosnia and Herzegovina, it is generally accepted that the government or local authorities have no obligation to help educate children before the age of six years, so the kindergartens are dependent on private funding. The area around Bijelo Polje had been ethnically cleansed during the war and it was only the presence of the Franciscan Sisters back in the area that gave the people the courage to return. The school was a huge attraction too.

Most people would not be able to afford the fees if they paid the correct amount of money, for unemployment, and therefore poverty, is high. The Sisters charge a minimal amount, enough to cover the basic expenses of food, heating, electricity and educational materials, but even that can be out of reach for some parents.

One small child was in a very difficult situation and the family could not pay the kindergarten any of the €100 a month fees. The mother had a job, but earned only €200 a month, therefore it was impossible for her to pay the fees. She could not give up the job to care for the child, for there is limited social security or state aid in Bosnia and Herzegovina. Only the poorest of the poor qualify for a welfare payment of €40 a month. Before he was born, the child's father had endured 16 years imprisonment after the war for a crime that would invite a sentence of one to two years in Western Europe. This situation creates a feeling of total injustice within the community. Lengthy prison sentences are handed out for what is considered to be petty crimes whilst the perception is that those who committed mass murder during the war receive little punishment. When a man comes out of prison, he is broken and it is extremely difficult for the family to re-establish itself as a unit even though married couples are sometimes allowed some intimate contact during the prison sentence. In this particular case, the little boy would start school within seven months and the Sisters approached St Joseph & The Helpers for help with funding his kindergarten fees. The charity agreed to guarantee the €700 required to cover the fees until the little one started school.

In October 2012, a group of visitors popped in to visit Sr Marija, Sr Dominika and the children of Bijelo Polje. The visit was enchanting and productive: enchanting because of the warm welcome and love emanating from the little kindergarten and productive, because one of the group members who had been busy with his camera for most of the visit, reached into his heart and offered to donate €2,500 for play equipment and landscaping the playground. A UK donor had already raised funds to purchase a children's slide. This is an example of the generosity of people who truly understand the needs of these dedicated Sisters and upon whom St Joseph & The Helpers depend on to continue their work in Bosnia and Herzegovina.

There is much work to do in Bijelo Polje and perhaps one day the old convent will stand in its former glory but this time as a Catholic secondary school for all in the area. At this time, the young children who are being nurtured by the Sisters can look forward to attending a state school but since the predominant religion is Islam in these parts, those who are Catholic will not have the opportunity to continue their Catholic education and formation other than within the family home.[12]

---

[12] For information on the work of the Sisters or how you can support this work, please refer to:
St Joseph & The Helpers Charity, www.helperscharity.com or contact:
Pat Henry, Chairman (UK) at pat@helperscharity.com
Tel: +44 (0) 144239107 ; Mob: +44 (0) 7866224671 or
Donal O'Shea, Director (UK) at donal@helperscharity.com
Tel: +353 (0) 12858130;   Mob. +353 (0) 872500424.

Chapter II

THE PRIEST and HIS PEOPLE

1.   Dezevice

Fr Slavisa's heart sank. He had waited for this moment for many years and now, one year after his ordination at the age of twenty-nine years, he had his very own parish.   As a young man, he had lived an exciting life in a materialistic world, but God had called him and he had answered that call with enthusiasm and total love. Now here he was, in winter, in a remote mountain village not far from Kiseljak; one that had been decimated of its youth during the Bosnian war and his Bishop was about to turn and leave him there.   His eyes travelled around the dilapidated house. It felt damp; the roof was leaking and the furniture sagged and groaned with age and despair. There was no running water, no heating, no working bathroom and even the mice were absent, most likely huddled in one small corner to escape the blast of the cold north wind.

The door closed.   He was alone.   Slowly, oh so slowly, he climbed the stairs, sat down on the edge of what was to be his bed and wept. Tears of disappointment saturated his coat.   How could he tell his parents?   How could he explain to them that their sacrifice had been for nothing?   The desolation seeped into his bones, smothering him in a dark blanket of despair and for what seemed like an age he sat motionless, drained of all energy, drained of hope.

Time passed. It seemed like an eternity. Slowly he stood up; slowly he walked downstairs, reached for the front door handle and stepped outside into the cold mountain air.   Hurriedly he ran to the church some thirty feet away and opened the door. An arctic blast of wind rushed from inside to greet him. How appropriate in a church called "Our Lady of the Snows". He stood paralysed. He felt crushed, helpless and painfully cold. Shivering, he wrapped his coat tightly around his thin body, fumbling to lift the corner of the lapel a little higher round his neck and ears and steadfastly he fixed his gaze on the large crucifix at the end of the sanctuary. With deliberation, he walked towards his God, stopped, head tilted, eyes brimming and quietly prayed the words, "Help me".

That night there was little sleep. He had eaten very little and the cold had snatched the warmth from his body. Wakening brought a new day to give light to his feelings of desolation. Where would he start? He tried to pray, but it was hard, he was cold and the whole situation was so difficult that prayer did not come easily. What could he do? His parishioners were elderly; they too had to struggle since there were no young people to help them, no one to care for them. Many had been killed during the Bosnian war; many had left the village forever during the ethnic cleansing, seeking a better life, leaving behind the old, alone, waiting to die in this little place called Dezevice. For two months, Fr Slavisa prayed and struggled and prayed, depression constantly at his side, refusing to leave, sucking the very life out of his soul. He could understand why his beloved Bishop had sent a young man with energy to tackle the problems but he was very lonely and he could not envisage how he could overcome the problems; it was a huge challenge to him.

Nearby in Kiseljak, Sr Jelenka heard of his plight. She understood his pain for she too had suffered greatly. Early in the Bosnian war, her family with along with many others, were ethnically cleansed from her home village of Dezevice and became refugees. Sr Jelenka's mother longed for her home, but it never happened and she died in exile only returning to Dezevice, much to the joy of her family, to be buried with her husband in the family plot next to the church. The war had destroyed families in the village, separating fathers from their wives and children all in the name of ethnicity or religion. Now in 2007, it was time for healing and this could only be done by re-energising the spirituality of the faithful parishioners whilst attracting the young back to the village. European monies had refurbished all the houses in the village, but not the presbytery or church and now Fr Slavisa had to somehow exist in these difficult circumstances whilst building and promoting growth in his parish.

Sr Jelenka moved quickly. St Joseph & The Helpers had built the kindergarten at Kiseljak and she felt confident that she could call on their generosity for this young priest. She had an ideal opportunity to introduce Arthur and Pat to Fr Slavisa when they came to stay at the Convent for the dedication ceremony of the Kindergarten on 16th October 2007.[1] That morning, with Sr Jelenka at the wheel, they set off with Sr Janja on the journey to the Alpine style village of Dezevice. Sr Jelenka is a very fast driver whom Arthur jokingly called Schumacher after the renowned international racing driver! Aided by Sr Janja to translate for all concerned, they learnt that Fr Slavisa was asking for their help to install heating in the Presbytery. There was a "range" type cooker in the main room which did not give out very much heat but there was no other heating in the house. Arthur and Pat could not help but notice that the house was in a terrible state of repair and they considered that the 'bathroom' should have been condemned. Fr Slavisa had arranged for the installation of new windows and a door for the church house but then his funds had run out.

They felt very sorry for the handsome young priest who felt terribly shy about asking for their financial help. Fr Slavisa explained that

---

[1] Pat Henry, Chairperson and Director of St Joseph & The helpers Charity (U.K) Ltd. Contact: pat@helperscharity.com. or St Joseph & The Helpers Charity (UK) Ltd, 12 Cangels Close, Hemel Hempstead, Herts, HP1 1NJ.

there were 1,000 parishioners in Dezevice before the war and now there were only 150 people in the village, 70 of those parishioners. His hope was that the people would return as there was a new 'water plant' in the village, the "Nevra" factory, where natural spring water was bottled. Ten young people were employed at the factory but if it expanded, he hoped more people would be employed and once more the village would increase in numbers. Shyly Fr Slavisa mentioned that a new roof was needed for the church house, but if they could do the heating now, perhaps he could ask for their help next year for the roof. He said that his aim was to make the Presbytery suitable for two priests and it was necessary therefore, to break through a third small bedroom and make a bathroom, shower room and separate toilet.

In their hearts, Pat and Arthur definitely wanted to help the young priest and informed him that they would put his project on their official charity website with the hope that people would want to support him, but they could not give any guarantees. This would have been enough had their hearts not been drawn to the plight of the parishioners, for Fr Slavisa then mentioned that the Church had no heating either. As Arthur and Pat stepped into the Church, they stood quietly, for it too, was in a very bad state of repair and already so cold even though it was only October. Pat joked with Fr Slavisa that he would have to give very short sermons or his parishioners would freeze to death, but in her heart she was already asking the question; how could they possibly walk away and leave this little community with its frail elderly people to struggle on in such difficult conditions? With determination, she turned to Arthur and announced that if they were seeking a quote for heating the Presbytery, they should include a quote for heating the Church; that would make the overall job more reasonably priced. Arthur said not a word, for his heart had also been touched by the plight of this little community and so he turned to Fr Slavisa and asked him to seek quotes for heating and also for refurbishing both buildings, the Church and the Presbytery.

Fr Slavisa could not believe what he was hearing. Excitement reverberated in the pit of his stomach and his face lit up in amazement. All his prayers were being answered. He was not alone; God had not deserted him, there was hope, and then, very quietly, he spoke to them in English. He was very shy about using this foreign language and his knowledge of it was very basic, but he felt pride and wanted to tell them how much he appreciated this wonderful and generous offer. They were unaware that he knew any English, but Arthur and Pat were moved at such monumental efforts to communicate with them and they were both deeply touched and humbled. Through the generosity of others, in time, St Joseph & The Helpers Charity would raise the necessary funds to have both buildings fully refurbished.

In 2007, the builders started work on the inside of the parish house. Arthur had suggested heating the church for the parishioners as the first priority, but what was the use of a warm church if the parish priest could not function due to the cold, so the parish house was renovated first! First, it was totally re-wired, insulated, plastered and painted. A wood-burning stove was installed to provide heating and hot water. Fr Slavisa reflected that before the work was undertaken, he could not have taken anyone to his house for there were no facilities to sit and talk, nowhere to pour a welcoming glass of "Orahovaca"[2]. Meanwhile the parishioners were still in the church freezing, "but they were used to it" reminisced Fr Slavisa, laughing out loud. Next, heating was installed in the church and then new doors were added. It was a huge improvement to keep out the Baltic

---

[2] Orahovaca is a local drink which is made from green walnuts, sugar, grape or plum brandy and grains of coffee. It is bottled and left in the sun for 30 days, shaken regularly, filtered, bottled and thoroughly enjoyed.

winds. The heating was installed in both the parish house and church in time for Christmas 2007 and for the first time, the parishioners had a beautiful, warm, Holy, Christmas. Fr Slavisa and his parishioners were very happy and very grateful.

In 2008 they started work on the outside of the parish house, first securing the roof, then the façade. They then started work on the church roof. The parishioners observed all of the activity in amazement and mulled that Fr Slavisa must be a little crazy. Where was all this money coming from? In spite of the appalling weather, with snow blocking the roads and the trucks carrying the necessary building materials unable to reach the village very easily, the Directors of St Joseph & The Helpers were amazed at the speed with which Fr Slavisa was able to achieve the work.

In late 2010 and early 2011, Fr Slavisa was back in communication with the charity asking for help with converting an outhouse into a Community Centre, to be used as a Pilgrim Centre. Many people make the pilgrimage to Jakov's (James or John) Holy Well, which is in a cave close to Dezevice church. "The people who come here" explains Fr Slavisa, "believe that the water will heal, especially the skin and eyes". Indeed Arthur himself had entered the cave in darkness and had walked straight into the water. At the time, Sr Jelenka had gone to visit her parents' graves alongside the church and when she returned she was faced with an embarrassed Arthur with soaking wet shoes and socks and an amused Sr Janja and Pat who could not contain their laughter. Fortunately, Sr Jelenka's brother lived nearby in the old family home and he generously gave Arthur some new socks and without complaining took Arthur's sodden socks in return.

A plaque near the entrance to the cave reads:

"St. James's life: he was born in 1394 in Monteprandone in Italy.[3] He finished law at a college in Perugia (Italy) and during his life wanted to become a Franciscan priest. The rest of his life he was a preacher around Europe and in his preaching he was pointing to the decline of modern society and in his own way he was showing the example of how to live as a true catholic. In 1432 he was named as Vicar of Bosnian Franciscans and he was in charge of religious education in Bosnia, but, because of the problems with the Bosnian King Tvrtko, he was soon sent back to his home in Italy. At the time of Pope Leon IV, he was back in Bosnia in 1435 and soon elected as a Bosnian visitor. St. James stayed in Bosnia until 1439 and he lived in the cave near to Dezevice. Bosnian Bishop Nickola Ogramich in the year of 1674 wrote about James in Dezevice. In 1899 the parish of Dezevice was rebuilt and James was proclaimed as their second guardian. [Our Lady of Snows is the first guardian, the second is James]. He died in 1476 in Napoli and Pope Benedict 13th proclaimed him as a saint in 1726. Today he is buried in a monastery in Monteprandone, his birth place."[4]

---

[3] Monteprandone is a commune in the Province of the Italian region Marche. It lies about 80 km southeast of Ancona which is on the Adriatic coast.

[4] Translated from original plaque by Adnan Safro (Translator) and Fr Slavisa.

On the first Sunday of each summer month, over 2,000 pilgrims make their way to the healing well where Mass is celebrated outdoors.   Fr Slavisa invites many priests to come and concelebrate the Mass and to hear confessions.   The people come from many miles away and bring the sick children who are blessed after Mass. Special prayers were sent from St James's birthplace in Italy and these are said when praying for the sick.

Stepping into the man-made cave, which is carved into the rock, is a timeless experience.   Like a comforting blanket, the small cave enfolds slowly round the visitor until soon the water from the well, invisible at first, creeps quietly to touch his feet.   It is customary to reach down and allow the water to lap over the face or hands and just for a time, the echo whispers back the prayers which are made in hope, then captures them and holds them firmly before they are released to Heaven.   Many people find it strange to think that St James would live in a place where there was water, but the mists of time have shaded the fading stories with myth and so it is said, 'Yes, James lived here'.

Stepping outside into the light, a shower of golden autumn leaves blows gently over the rock altar where Mass is celebrated, and settles softly on the wooden benches which seat the thousands of pilgrims, ascending into the forest above. Peace whispers its way through this Holy place, bringing hope to the little village whose future is tied with the constancy of the pilgrims.   "The Shrine is the future of the village" declares Fr Slavisa, "that is why the pilgrim (pastoral) centre is so important".

It is not quite finished, but the centre stands proudly near the church, built as they do in Austria with sloping roof, prepared for the snow which can lie up to 1.5 metres at any time.   "There will be three apartments," smiles Fr Slavisa, "two or three beds per place, one for six beds, and so up to ten or twelve places for the pilgrims". The project is exciting. There will be a kitchen, a bathroom and a public toilet outside and a little room for meetings, for social gatherings, for just being together.

The little dirt road used to run in front of where the centre now sits, in between the presbytery and the church, leading to the beautiful mountain cemetery where Sr Jelenka's parents rest peacefully. Fr Slavisa built a new road running behind the centre so that cars can carry the old people who find it difficult to walk the one hundred metres to pay their respects to their loved ones. Mass is said two or three times a year in the cemetery, to pay respects to the dead and the little gravestones are smothered in rich colourful flowers from the village gardens.

A statue of 'Our Lady of the Snows' stands outside the five steps leading to the large wooden doors of the Church, framed in a concrete arc, overshadowed by a cross and a window in the shape of a 'host', adjoining the tower which holds the bell calling all the parishioners to prayer. Inside, at the far end of the church, three marble steps lead to the Sanctuary where the altar is framed by two simple arched windows each adorned with a stained glass golden cross. Flowers are placed lovingly at the foot of the altar in reverence, respect and showing colour and life. To the right of the altar, stand proudly the Easter candle and the lectern adorned in green cloth. Leading down from the Sanctuary and to the right, lies the relic of St James of Monteprandone, which came to Dezevice from his shrine in Italy. It is protected by a glass box, sitting next to his bronze statue. His body is kept in the monastery of Monteprandone where he was born and buried. Since St James lived for a time in Dezevice as an apostolic visitor, the people of Dezevice are connected with the Italians. So at Fr Slavisa's request, the Italians donated the relic in honour of that relationship, in August 2011. To the left of the Sanctuary, the parishioner can kneel quietly and pray at the foot of a statue of Mary, the mother of Jesus. The church is simple, beautiful with pine benches; light beams into every window and the church interior sparkles in the sunlight with a quiet dignity.

In September 2011, a month after Arthur had died, Fr Slavisa contacted the charity again to inform them that the work had been completed but the Pilgrim Centre was very cold as they had no money to put in windows or heating! He had hoped that they could complete the project so that the Pilgrim Centre would be ready for Spring 2012.[5] Arthur had informed Fr Slavisa on several occasions that the charity did not have any money for all these extra projects, but Fr Slavisa, in faith, just kept on updating the charity about the work in progress. In God's world, His timing is perfect and nothing is by chance, for at the time Fr Slavisa was completing the project, the charity received a very generous donation and so €25,000 was paid to Fr Slavisa to complete the job. Pat reflects warmly, "Arthur would be smiling right now, knowing that Fr Slavisa got his way in the end."[6]

---

[5] The project completion was delayed due to severe snow storms which swept through Bosnia and Herzegovina in February 2012 and a state of emergency was declared. Note: With regard to future retreats and/or use of the centre, the Parish Priest can be contacted on: **Telephone: +387-30-804-715.** In 2012 the Bishop moved Fr Slavisa to another parish.

[6] Total costs to date (2012) : 2007: Parish House and Church renovations and refurbishments - €18,618.
2008: Parish House Roof - €15,029; Church Roof - €15,000. 2011: Pastoral Centre - €25,000. Heating costs paid by the charity to date: €7,200. Total: €80,847. This was made possible by the generous donations given to St Joseph & The Helpers Charity.

2. Zenica – St Joseph Parish

Fr Slavisa did not stop when his own needs were met; so many of his fellow priests were suffering in similar conditions and he yearned to help those, if he could, as he was being helped in such a favourable way. Arthur was sure that there were many priests who were suffering in similar conditions and it was difficult to walk away from these stalwart Shepherds of the Flock. Consideration would be given to each and every request that came their way.

In September 2008, St Joseph & The Helpers Charity received a letter from Fr Vladimir Prankić, parish priest of St Joseph's Church in Zenica which is located about 70 km (43 miles) north of Sarajevo and according to locals, is the fourth largest city in Bosnia and Herzegovina. This prompted Arthur to visit Fr Vladimir on his next trip to Bosnia and Herzegovina and confirm the condition of the house reported in Fr Vladimir's letter:

"Vrhbosanka nadbiskupija Zenica, 25 September 2008.
Župni ured sv. Josipa,
Strossmayerova 17,
BiH-72000 Zenica.
Tel/fax. 032/462-106; email: vladimirp@net.hr

Dear Sirs,

Appeal for aid in rebuilding parish office and parish home in parish St. Joseph in Zenica

On the recommendation of Reverend Slaviša S. parish priest in Deževice, and unable to realize the projects for lack of funds, I apply to you for the help.

I am parish priest in the parish St. Joseph in Zenica, appointed on July 25, 2008.

The parish had approximately 10,000 believers before the war, but during and after the war two thirds of parishioners left their homes in search of better life.

So today the parish has only 2,650 believers in 850 families, 70% of whom are pensioners. The other 30% of people are young families. We are trying to hold them all in this area. This parish is their shelter and hope that it will be better tomorrow. They gather here and make each other stronger in every day survival.

When I came to this parish, I realized that it needs serious renovation. In the past ten years parish church has been renovated from both inside and outside so it is more beautiful and warmer space nowadays for the believers to pray and celebrate God.

But the parish house is in very difficult state. It is forty years old and almost nothing on it has ever been renewed. The roof lets water in some places, and it doesn't have any insulation. The carpentry is in the same condition. And last of all, I would like to make the interior more pleasant and comfortable to spend time in.

Considering the economical power of parishioners, most of whom are senior citizens, and their contributions, I am sure you understand that it is impossible to realize this project on my own. There are also Ursuline sisters in this parish, that Ursuline convent is the only one in Bosnia and Herzegovina. Four sisters live there, and three of them are retired from active service. Their house is also in very difficult state, but it is partly included in renovation, the roof, façade, carpentry. The company Seting d.d. Žepče draw up an estimate of all construction work to the amount of €82,000.

Considering all, I am forced to ask for the help of good people. Because of that I ask you to become part of this humane effort and help me according to your abilities.

Yours faithfully,
Reverend Vladimir Prankić,, parish priest.

I enclose: 1. List of expenses.
2. Picture of Current state."

When Arthur visited the parish house, he was introduced to a young priest called Fr Simo Marsic who had come to translate for Fr Vladimir. The house was just as the pictures showed. So much was in a dilapidated state, with little privacy for Fr Vladimir in amongst the Ursuline Sisters. Arthur was touched by the priest's plight and felt sorry for him, especially when he saw that the Sisters also used Fr Vladimir's parish house to hang up their washing on the days when it was wet outside; and so it was, that St Joseph & The Helpers pledged €20,000 to Fr Vladimir to help convert his ageing parish house and convent to a place that was fitting for these dedicated souls.

Father's delight at receiving such a gift touched Arthur once more and when St Joseph & The Helpers received yet another request from the parish priest at Prozor Rama located in the northern parts of Herzegovina-Neretva Canton, he did not hesitate to persuade his directors to send €10,000 to help with the renovation works of the parish house.

54

How many more, he thought, suffer the indignity of living in impoverished conditions? Arthur reflected on his native Ireland where it was normal for the parish priest to be taken care of materially to a standard that was acceptable throughout Europe. He wondered how these conditions in Bosnia and Herzegovina impacted on their faith; did it strengthen the faith, did it weaken the faith? He did not know. He only knew that through St Joseph & The Helpers, God had given him, the directors and all the helpers, an opportunity to throw a life-line both materially and psychologically to these precious priests.[7]

---

[7] If you wish to know more about how you can help the priests in Bosnia and Herzegovina, please go to the St Joseph & The Helpers Charity website at St Joseph & The Helpers Charity, www.helperscharity.com or contact:
Pat Henry, Chairman (UK) at pat@helperscharity.com
Tel: +44 (0) 144239107 ; Mob: +44 (0) 7866224671 or
Donal O'Shea, Director (UK) at donal@helperscharity.com
Tel: +353 (0) 12858130; Mob. +353 (0) 872500424.

Chapter III

THE FAMILY

1. Mother's Village, Bijakovici, Medjugorje.

Fr Svetozar Kraljevic (Fr. Svet) noticed the man walking towards him and stopped briefly to talk to him. "Do you need anything here at Mother's Village?" the man enquired. Fr Svet glanced at this tall rugged man cautiously; many men came to Medjugorje; many offered their help but at times the offer of help was transient, unfulfilled and left abandoned. Fr Svet frowned, looked at him intently. "Yes," he replied. "We need many things; we need food for our children, shoes for their feet and education." Words were not necessary. Many years had passed since their first meeting. "His mother had come to the confessional" reminisces Fr Svet; "she had a great faith. He waited patiently for her and we exchanged warm salutations. Time had passed, his faith had deepened, he was a shrewd businessman, but his way had changed. He wanted to help us."

Fr Slavko Barbaric was a Franciscan priest in the parish of Medjugorje from the early days of the alleged visions of Our Blessed Mother. It has been many years since Fr Slavko had cleared the tangled bushes, debris and waste from the land, many years since little family houses accommodating six to eight children were built to provide protection and care for the children who suffered the loss of their homes and parents during the cruel war. Now, since Fr. Slavko's death, it was left to Fr Svet to provide for these children. Help is much needed. Fr Svet struggles with the daily task of feeding, clothing and educating the children. How many children had come his way, some so broken they did not speak. Others cried for nights on end, but they came. First, during the war; then after the war;

and now, as a result of the war. Sixteen years had passed since the war ended, but progress was slow and the country remained ravaged and torn, struggling to survive in a global political and economic environment. As in many countries which had suffered the pains of war, unemployment, poverty, despair and resulting alcoholism pushed families to destruction in Bosnia and Herzegovina. In the early days, many children had arrived at Mother's Village unwanted, without hope and abandoned. Many had lost everything, had no one left to care for them, and many had suffered such deep trauma, that physical and mental pain had become a constant companion.

But Fr Svet had prayed, knowing that it would take a miracle to ensure that every child was fed, had a pair of shoes on his/her feet, had the help they required to overcome their deep-rooted nightmares and eventually to achieve that important diploma in school which would enable them to step into the future with confidence.[1] He also knew that the same miracle had to extend to care for his workers – they too were victims, many limping to Mother's Village in despair but with the hope of a job, companionship and dignity. How good it felt to have dignity, to feel that what you did was important, necessary, and that you could feed your family. There is very little state aid to depend on, limited government handouts and work is extremely hard to find. This is a country of intelligent, talented people who have much to offer; much to give, not only to their own community but to the world. Teachers, psychologists, psychiatrists, doctors,

---

[1] It takes approx €50 per month to cover all costs for one child at Mother's Village. If you wish to donate, please go to:
St Joseph & The Helpers Charity, www.helperscharity.com or contact:
Pat Henry, Chairman (UK) at pat@helperscharity.com
Tel: +44 (0) 144239107 ; Mob: +44 (0) 7866224671 or
Donal O'Shea, Director (UK) at donal@helperscharity.com
Tel: +353 (0) 12858130;   Mob. +353 (0) 872500424.

nurses, pharmacists, computer experts, builders, engineers, librarians, drivers, scientists, all live in the hope of finding that one important job, but without that job, the desperation of being unemployed eats into their very souls, robbing them of sleep, cheating them of living as decent human beings.

There are many children at Mother's Village, approximately 55 at any given time; in fact, after the war in Yugoslavia 500,000 children were displaced, made homeless or had suffered the loss of one or both of their parents. The war had devastated their lives. Their Mums and Dads were gone. They came to Mother's Village as babies, their brothers and sisters were older but they had now moved on to jobs or university. Mother's Village had been their home, their refuge, after the war and it had not been easy for them. Some had witnessed their family members gunned down in front of them. One little boy hid beneath a wood pile; he couldn't cry and he couldn't understand why; but someone took his hand and carried his sister in their arms and brought them here to Mother's Village. At first they were very afraid, but they loved the little family houses and the warm smells of cooking. It made them feel safe and reminded them of home for in each house there were no more than eight children and two "mothers" to care for them. When he first came, Ivan secured the job of feeding the kitten. He used to have a kitten but it too had gone, burnt with the old dog when they burnt the house down.

Although the war is now over, the social aftermath fed by unemployment and alcoholism has resulted in problems which have no immediate solutions. Now the children come for different reasons, but all require the same safety, love and protection. They come because they are children in need. They come because Mother's Village offers them a chance in life to grow, to become confident, to be educated before branching out into the wider community.

Life in Mother's Village is good; there is a Kindergarten which is attended by 160 children consisting of the children of Mother's Village and the local children. There is a little chapel, a huge fruit and vegetable garden, a little shop which sells the many items made by the community. The lonely German Shepherd dog waits patiently. In time he will be let out of his pen and perhaps they will let him play with one of the other dogs. The children's shrills carry from St Francis Garden and, reverberating across the hills, can be heard all over Mother's Village. The ponies were being naughty but they needed to be fed. Some had come as unwanted and abandoned animals in a very poor state, but the children knew exactly how they felt. They knew how important it was to know that each day they would be fed; they understood the joy of having a warm, clean place to live and the healing power of an unconditional hug, a kiss, that intimate communication with another being. So they willingly fetched the hay and the grain and they would never abandon the ponies. It had been Fr Slavko's idea to have the animals. He knew that they would teach the children how to love unconditionally, how to be compassionate and responsible towards the care of another being. He knew that if the children learned love through the animals, they would soon learn to love each other. Perhaps, then, there would be no more fighting in the country, just people living together in harmony and peace.

St Joseph's Community Hall

Fr Svet had just come down from the mountain. He noticed Arthur strolling towards him. Arthur stopped, greeted Fr Svet warmly and enquired how things were at Mother's Village.

59

"Do you need anything more here at Mother's Village?" he asked. Fr Svet looked at him intently. "I have a dream", he responded. "We need a hall, a hall of our own, but we have no money."

"You go ahead with your plan Father; decide what you want. You build the hall and we will find the money", suggested Arthur.

"I must confess", muses Fr Svet, "it was made like this in five to six minutes and then we went on our way." The building eventually cost Arthur's charity €561,648 which included €40,000 for the air-conditioning units. The money was sent directly to the building company with no administration charges, no fees and no hassle for Mother's Village which delighted Fr Svet!

Prior to his untimely death Fr Slavko Barbaric had discussed the need for this Centre with Fr Svet who tells us that it was Fr Slavko's dream and that it became his dream too. He writes:

"Dear Friend,

This multi-purpose building will include a small chapel of 200 sq. metres and another 1,000 sq. metres in the hall. It is for all the community to share but especially for the children of Medjugorje Parish and the people in our drug rehabilitation programme. Our pilgrims will also have a better ministry and can celebrate services from the Church, especially at New Year and other busy times. There is no similar hall in Medjugorje and it will be wonderful for the teachers and children to enjoy sports, art activities, drama and Christmas plays – that everyone can attend. I place this project, like all projects in

*Mother's Village, into the Providence of Our Lord Jesus
and into the Hands of Our Lady.*

I welcome you to be part of this Providence.

***Pax et bonum
Fr Svetozar Kraljevic"***

A few of the boys come and ask, "Father, can we play in the
hall?" The hall is finished and the new sports floor gleams in
the light. Arthur never saw the final completion, his death
crept into the time-scale and others would stand in his place in
awe of all that had been achieved. It's used for basketball,
sometimes soccer, concerts, meetings, talks, just like any other
normal community hall. It is also available to the local
community and children of the local schools. "A cafeteria
would be good" suggests Donal, "right there attached to the
hall."[2] His idea was that people would come, look around
Mother's Village, have a cup of coffee, and watch a DVD on
the work of the charity. At the nearby sculpture of the Risen
Christ, they will be able to reflect on the remembrance plaque
that will one day acknowledge Arthur's love, his commitment
which provided the foundation stones for St Joseph's Hall.
Arthur wouldn't like the fuss; he was humble, shy and would
only want honour for the Mother of Jesus or Jesus himself, but
he would be pleased to know that the generosity and hard work
of the Helpers was being recognised through the memorial
plaque which would encourage others to continue the work.

---

[2] Donal O'Shea, Director (UK), St Joseph & The Helpers. Email:
donal@helperscharity.com

The 'Merciful Father': Healing for Addicts

For God cares, especially for those who have no hope, who have reached the very bottom of the pile – a dark cave with its own devouring demons of addiction. How many have stumbled, staggered and crawled, devoid of life, hope and love, to the gates of Mother's Village, and into the arms of the "Merciful Father" but with the knowledge that each step would take him or her to the foot of the mountain of recovery.

Arthur knew and understood their pain; hadn't he been there himself, drowning in the lie of champagne disguised as happiness; soaring on the self-indulgence of gambling? What could he give back? He himself had been grabbed dramatically from the river of self-destruction; he knew the struggle of addiction and desperation. How many more could come this way to Mother's Village and the "Merciful Father" if only they had more help. The bills had to be paid, the construction cement for the building projects had to be purchased, the dish-washing liquid, the food; all to be bought. Thank goodness for the vegetables, the fruit, the pigs, the chickens, but what about the men and women themselves, their souls, their dignity? They had to be nourished, had to have hope, had to see God in action; that they too were important, that their lives meant something.

So Arthur talked – he talked to groups, to individuals, in Medjugorje, in Ireland, in Scotland and England, in the USA; wherever he had the chance to talk, he talked, and as he talked, the scales fell from their eyes as they realised that this could be their brother, father, husband, son, daughter, sister, wife, mother and that they too could help. Being a 'Helper' meant nothing more than making one prayer to God, giving one euro or helping with the fund-raising so that others could give; but it was the giving, of self, of time, of resources that was important.

So they followed Arthur's example and gave; some a little, some much, but each was an offering, a sacrifice to the Lord who in turn whispered in the ears of each addict, "You are worth it. I gave MY life for YOU. We will never forget you."

The sound of victory echoed throughout the hall. It was no ordinary football game. This was serious. The 'stand' proudly displayed bottles of water, snacks, the 'money' tin – well you might win, you might lose, but you still have to pay! This was their hall; this was from the Helpers, from those who cared. It wasn't empty words, imaginations, dreams – you could touch it, feel it, run in it, shout, scream and jump, but it was theirs. Tomorrow the girls would commandeer the space; battered and bruised, mentally and physically, but they too were healing. What better way to become lean and strong, fit and healthy and give vent to those pent up emotions that had been robbed by the comatose state of addiction.

As each day dawned, the young men had to be ready, first for prayer, then for breakfast and then work. Work took on many guises, for the daily chores of any household, washing, cooking, cleaning, was only part of the activity at Mother's Village. The workshop provides a necessary focus for the shattered minds of the young addicts and as they heal, their spirits soar in the freedom of expression and the most beautiful handmade wooden crosses, paintings, and other precious crafts are produced and sold. The sales support the young men in buying the provisions that are needed to live; that and the garden which is tended in peace by those whose bodies are slowly recovering from the wreckage of addiction. In turn the produce will restore weak muscles, build strong bones, and nourish maltreated beings to bring them to a state of vibrancy and strength. Harvesting the grapes, feeding the chickens and pigs; all become part of the daily routine. In addition, there are buildings to be built, roofs to repair, fences to erect and time measured exactly so that thanksgiving can be given to God for the chance to live again.

The noise grew louder as the opposition scored yet another goal and shouts of frustration could be heard in amongst jubilation as the game reached yet another crescendo. Soon it would be time to cool down, enjoy the feast of victory, but right now the battle was still raging in St Joseph's Hall. Suddenly it was all over, the lights switched off and the doors closed firmly. Night prayer and precious sleep awaited them and unlike the nightmare of past times, the assurance of another new day lay ahead.

In the women's house, the night is also drawing to a close. Addiction takes its own forms in the precious bodies of sensitive women. Many had lost their children, taken from them as they were unable to care for them; many had experienced the depravity of prostitution to feed the hungry habit of drugs and alcohol and many had been rejected by friends, by family, by society, as useless leeches and not worthy of life. Yet these were the daughters of some family and they had started life as innocent children. These were the young women with hearts full of yearning, dreams, ambition, and hope for the future; who had stumbled onto the wrong path only to find themselves trapped in a dangerous snare of poisonous venom. How easy it is to take the wrong road, but how difficult it is to find a way to the path of life.

What drives a woman to seek solace in the numbing bed of alcohol or drugs? Where are the people in her life who should be protecting her, guarding her and caring for her? No one takes this path by choice, no one chooses to numb the pain with cheap alcohol and drugs; only circumstances and the easiness with which these substances are available tempt the woman to consume in secret until slowly, she looks in the mirror and is faced with the wretchedness of her condition; dry wrinkled skin tortured by dehydration, limp lifeless hair, eyes filled with sorrow and desperation, violent shakes in the early morning and a slow death; a slow, lingering death as the body finally breaks down.

How wrong they are to think that they are worthless, how wrong they are to think that they do not matter. Their lives are as precious to God as all the other lives in the world, even more so because theirs is fragile and on the brink of extinction. And so it is, with providence and fortitude, they find themselves in Mother's Village; safe in a house provided by the generosity of others who do care, who want these beautiful women to return to the bosom of society, for they have much to contribute. Their experience, their journey is so vital to others and as they recover, they can reach out and help those who have not yet found the road to life. For without this safe haven in Mother's Village, the road ahead leads to destruction and death.

Daily Life

The mini-van zooms past and two of the women wave at the visitors. They are off to do some kitchen work, helping to feed the children. It is a beautiful crisp autumn day and whilst the sun is shining, there is just a hint with the cool breeze that winter is not too far away. The children will be in school today, but there is work to be done in Mother's Village, projects to complete and so the men and the women who have found life in this place are busy planning the day to include cement and bricks, gardening, cooking, washing, feeding the chickens and pigs and all the chores of everyday life.

The shop is open and the visitor enters into a paradise of innovation, colour and genius as a book is chosen, a painting is gazed upon and a Rosary is carefully lifted up to the sunlight. The aroma of fruit candles lingers gently in the little shop allowing a sense of timelessness and tranquillity in the humdrum of the day. A little cat winds its way around the legs, searching for the next person to lift her up and give the attention she so enjoys and there is delight in the lingering of just a moment to enjoy each purrrr of contentment.

This is a place of family where each person has a place in the family and where each person's contribution, no matter how big or small is important for the body of the family. There is much pride in the achievements in Mother's Village, but for the visitor, there is so much love radiating from the stones and gravel of the red coloured earth. The surrounding mountains guard, protecting favourably the enclave of hope and so it is that another day starts in Mother's Village. A day just like any other day, but where the throbbing of life beats harmoniously in rhythm to the prayers, laughter and hope of the renewed spirits.

Each day the money to care for all those who live there must be found by the Director of Mother's Village. He has no income except through the donations of generous helpers. Salaries have to be paid and 300 meals have to be provided every day. Fr Svet says "we need a miracle every month just to survive." He trusts God to touch the hearts of those who can give and depends totally on providence. All those who come to Mother's Village are transformed.[3]

---

[3] Donations to Mother's Village can be given through:
St Joseph & The Helpers Charity, www.helperscharity.com or contact:
Pat Henry, Chairman (UK) at pat@helperscharity.com
Tel: +44 (0) 144239107 ; Mob: +44 (0) 7866224671 or
Donal O'Shea, Director (UK) at donal@helperscharity.com
Tel: +353 (0) 12858130;   Mob. +353 (0) 872500424.

2. The Children: John Paul II Orphanages in Citluk and Vionica

Near to Mother's Village in Bijakovici, lie the hamlets of Vionica, Surmanci and Miletina, all part of the Parish of Medjugorje which is part of Citluk municipality. Two orphanages run by Sr Kornelijie snuggle into the terrain of Citluk and Vionica, John Paul II, No. 1 at Citluk and John Paul II, No. 2 at Vionica. Walking into either of the orphanages the visitor is showered with a rainbow of colours, light and laughter integrated with the hustle and bustle of a busy family life. Like any family home, there is a routine and like any routine, it sometimes does not work. Amidst the laughter there are squabbles, tears, intimate discussions, dolls, teddy bears, washing, ironing, lunch, dinner, prayers and sleep. People come and people go; aromas of the most exquisite kind drift from the kitchen and the old cat crosses into the parlour on forbidden territory.

Many of the children arrive at the orphanages traumatised, scared, silent, unwilling to share any of their feelings except those giveaway tears, but within a few days, they submerge into the normality of family life, healing, laughing, just like any normal child the world over. They stay at the orphanage until they are eighteen years old, studying at school, involved in community life and growing in their faith.

At Vionica orphanage the visitor enters the gate and is first greeted with a beautiful bronzed statue of a woman adorned with small children, a reassuring presence of the love that the child will find within the garden gates. Next to the statue, a cool air whispers invitingly from the little Church, beckoning the weary traveller to sit at the foot of the statue of Christ and bathe in the serenity of harmony, stillness and peace. Quiet contemplation follows, reflection, meditation, thoughtful insights, uniting the bronze statue to the living Christ and the children within.   All are welcome and no one is turned away. Many return as young adults, to give to the little ones the same love that they received.

The children are not just forgotten when they reach eighteen years of age; the Sisters help them to find work or funding for training. One young man was about to leave the orphanage and go to live in Croatia with his uncle where he would learn how to make bread. One young girl was helped by the Sisters to train as a hairdresser and they helped her find a house so that she was able to accommodate her younger siblings.

 In 2006, Arthur recognised the needs of another young girl, writing:

"The Girl with a Beautiful Heart" by Arthur McCluskey (Winter 2007)

"On a pilgrimage to Medjugorje in September 2006, I met a young girl during our group's visit to the Orphanage in Vionica. As we were leaving to get on the bus, I noticed that she was crying and had a great look of sadness on her face. She was with a man and woman who I assumed were her parents and that she wanted to go home with them. Out of sympathy and to console her, I gave her a €20 note and said that I would come back to see her. Another member of our group was also taking in the scene but I was unaware of this until I received a letter from him shortly after we returned home. He included a very generous cheque and said, "I was watching the scene with misty eyes and you have to look after that girl."

And so on my next visit I set out to find her. I very quickly established that she was in the Citluk Orphanage which is only a short distance away from Vionica. I invited my friend Wayne Weible to join me and we called to the Orphanage with a lady called Rosa as our interpreter. Lydia is a 13 year old Serbian girl from Banja Luka, which is some five hours drive away.[4] I learnt that my assumption was wrong about the two people with her that first day. They were, in fact, two social workers who had taken her from the only home she knew to a life in an orphanage. Little wonder at her sadness and tears that first day in Vionica.

As we gently tried to establish her background, Lydia told us that her 51 year old mother had died three years earlier and her alcoholic father died some eight months ago at the age of sixty-three years. He had been married twice and she had a step-brother who was married. They all lived together along with her mother's sister, in the same house.

Tensions were running high so Lidjia and her Aunt were evicted. As they had nowhere to go, government officials stepped in and took Lydia to Sr Kornelijie's Orphanage where she was welcomed with open arms and love. Now her tears were flowing again – but not for herself. This girl with a beautiful heart was only concerned for the well-being of her Aunt. "How will she live; who will take care of her and where will she go?" Questions to which we had no answers. Wayne and I were now in tears as this beautiful compassionate girl opened her heart to us. Wayne

---

[4] The girl's name changed for reasons of confidentiality.

whispered to me through the tears, "they never forget the pain" as he recalled his own personal experience.

We left promising to visit her as often as possible and, thank God, life is looking far brighter for her now. I introduced my good friend Vesna Radisic from Medjugorje to Lydia and they now love one another. Her Aunt's situation has also improved as the local authorities found her a home. Lydia was able to visit her for a holiday during this summer so she is very happy now. She has thirteen subjects to study at school and karate is her favourite sport. Lydia prays constantly to our blessed mother and on one of my visits she shared that she was hoping to become a religious sister. More recently boys were her favourite subject – a perfectly normal adolescent young lady."

Through Vesna Radisic, Arthur remained in contact with Lydia until he died in 2011. If he had the opportunity to glimpse into Lydia's life at this moment in time, he would feel nothing but pride; she has grown into a fine young lady. She is now settled as a hairdresser and has set up her own hairdressing business in her home where she is reunited with her younger siblings. Sr Kornelija paid for Lydia's hairdressing course and equipment and helped her find a place to call home. Lydia is one of thousands of young people leaving the orphanages who need that support, to gain the skills and qualifications for work and business.

In 2008, St Joseph & The Helpers refurbished the local school at Vionica which is attended by the very young children from the Orphanage. The external walls had never been plastered and the internal walls had blackened due to damp, causing several of the children to contact severe respiratory problems.

The school was restored at a cost of €7,500 Euros and the difference to the children's health was immediate.

There are still many orphans in Bosnia and Herzegovina; as in other countries throughout the world, babies continue to be abandoned when the adults are damaged psychologically and unable to cope. It is often difficult to know the best way to help. In 2008, St Joseph & The Helpers were asked to find sponsorship for over 700 orphans, with limited success. However, this strategy may be the best way forward. In today's world, where recessions are biting many families who once had much to spare and gave generously, perhaps it is best to ask oneself, can we take care of one more child in our family? If the answer is yes, let us give to the child in Bosnia and Herzegovina who has no mother, no father and no future without our help. Any donation to an Orphanage through St Joseph & The Helpers would be gratefully received.[5]

3.   The daughter: Little Lucija

Nearby in Mostar, a little girl is unable to attend kindergarten, but is not an orphan; she is one of the fortunate children in Bosnia and Herzegovina who has been born into a loving, caring family. Lucija was born in Mostar in January 2001 as a premature baby. Due to her early birth and perhaps the birth

---

[5] It costs an estimated £40 or €50 Euros per month (£1.30 or €1.7 per day) to cover all the costs of feeding, clothing and educating one young child.
Support for the kindergartens and orphanages can be give through:
St Joseph & The Helpers Charity, www.helperscharity.com or contact:
Pat Henry, Chairman (UK) at pat@helperscharity.com
Tel: +44 (0) 144239107 ; Mob: +44 (0) 7866224671 or
Donal O'Shea, Director (UK) at donal@helperscharity.com
Tel: +353 (0) 12858130; Mob. +353 (0) 872500424.

process itself, some of her body functions were severely damaged.

The family are committed to helping little Lucija and since the early days of her existence, each member has been intensively involved in a programme of exercising her muscles to enable her to stand. However, her young parents were told that there is no hope for Lucija and that there is a huge possibility that she will never be able to walk. Since she and the family are determined to continue with the programme, even if she never walks she will always need some form of walking aid and transport to ensure that she can be included in all the family activities.

To the family's utmost joy, in 2006, St Joseph & The Helpers provided Lucija with a new buggy which was specially adapted to her needs and fitted to ensure that she sat comfortably and could interact with her sister Ana who is two years older.

Lucija's family are in a position where they can take care of her, but many children do not have a loving family to nourish them and care for them. There are many needs in Bosnia and Herzegovina but the family home, the kindergartens and the orphanages are the garden beds where the future generation will grow in strength together.

4. The Mother

Vjekoslzv and Ornella married in Mostar in 1995 and a year later whilst giving birth to twin boys, Ornella went into a coma. She remained in hospital until 2007 when the Municipality of Mostar gave them an apartment. St Joseph & The Helpers adapted and refurbished the apartment at a cost of €8,250, so that Ornella could be taken to live at home. Unfortunately,

Ornella never regained consciousness and very sadly she died in 2012, having never seen her beautiful sons.

Whilst the story is tragic, there is a great deal to be thankful for in Ornella's life. She was loved throughout her life by her husband Vjekoslav. She may have been aware of that love, for her level of consciousness was undetermined, but the most important thing is that her sons had the opportunity to live in the same house as their mother.

The apartment was refurbished to a high standard, taking into consideration the detail required to ensure that Ornella could be nursed and taken care of without difficulty. It must have brought great comfort to her family and friends, knowing that someone they loved was in their midst, safe and secure. Without the generosity of the Helpers, Ornella and her family would never have had the opportunity to turn a tragedy into something beautiful. This has helped Vjekoslav and the boys heal and come to terms with the loss of a beautiful wife and a beautiful mother, Ornella.

5. The Father: Shovel

'Shovel' (a nick-name), a gentle Muslim, stood patiently at the corner of the street on a daily basis, hoping to catch the eye of the 'man with the money' who would hire him for one day's work. His shovel, his only tool and the umbilical cord that enabled his large family to be nourished, was sharpened each evening in preparation for the daily ritual on the street corner. In the early hours of each day, often in the dark, as he strapped his thin coat around his emaciated body to shield himself from the bitter northerly winds, Shovel stood like a sentry on duty waiting for his opportunity to work. He was a proud man who held his weary body with dignity, but often had to stem the waves of desperation and despair as he turned to go home after hours of waiting, unhired, unwanted, and unable to provide for his six children.

It had been a very difficult time for Shovel and his family and the grief was etched on his face as a permanent reminder of what he had endured. One day during the war, a soldier deliberately threw a grenade at one of Shovel's little children, a little boy of eight years of age. The little boy thought it was a ball, something to play with and leaned over happily to catch it in his hands. The explosion was deafening as the little boy's body tore apart into a thousand pieces under the impact.

'Shovel' was in detention at the time his son was killed and he pleaded to be released temporarily to go to his son's funeral.[6] Instead his jailers beat him up, knocked his teeth out and put him into solitary confinement, taunting him at every opportunity, opening a wound that would never close.

After the war, one soldier was identified and brought to The Hague to be put on trial for war crimes. The soldier's father offered 'Shovel' a bribe of $25,000 not to testify. Shovel's response to him was, "is that all my son's life is worth?" In total disgust, Shovel refused to take one cent from the man. Instead, his testimony convicted his son's killer to his rightful punishment.

Shovel and his family were living in very difficult circumstances, in a house that was in poor condition. Through the generosity of others, he was able to build a new house, one in which his family could live in dignity. His daily search for work continued until one day Matthew Procter from 'Miracles Charity' gave him an idea. Mathew had sustained him and

---

[6] Like many people at that time, Shovel had been incarcerated unjustly.

74

helped him through the difficulties of going to The Hague and testifying against his son's killer. Matthew suggested that Shovel contact Arthur to see if the charity he was working with at the time, "Rebuild for Bosnia", could help him purchase a truck. This would enable Shovel to be self-employed and to give his sons the work they desperately needed.[7] Arthur, in his true compassionate way, immediately realised the necessity and opportunity to help this dignified man and his family.

The day the truck was delivered to Shovel was one of the happiest days of his life. However, he never forgot the kindness and generosity of others and in return Shovel has reached out to help many who are also in difficult circumstances.

6. The Widow

Climbing to the place of the Blue Cross is one of the most exhilarating walks for the enthusiastic pilgrim and on reaching a little Pensione, just a stone's throw away from the site of the Blue Cross is a neat little house with a welcoming veranda where the pilgrim can relax and enjoy a refreshing glass of lemonade in the heat of the day.

A welcome smile radiates from a beautiful young woman as she proudly shows the pilgrim her sparkling clean dining room leading to the coolness of the bedrooms upstairs. She was young and had two young children when her husband committed suicide. There was no warning, no suicide note and no indication that his depression had reached the depths of a vortex, too dark to contemplate. He had never recovered from

---

[7] 'Rebuild for Bosnia': Arthur worked for this charity for four years, prior to founding St Joseph & The Helpers.

the effects of the war. It haunted him day and night and ate into his dreams, his waking moments, his leisure time, his work time and even his beautiful wife and children could not shut out the nightmares.

Left alone, suddenly, she had no means of support and no way to feed her children, herself and her mother-in-law who lived with her. She did not know which way to turn. A friend put her in touch with St Joseph & The Helpers and for the next few years, the charity were able to pay her a monthly "pension", a life-saver, to help the widow and her family survive. She had to cope with the grief on her own and she had to care for the children and her mother-in-law, but she had no prospect of finding a job. She wanted to help herself and she wanted to be independent and so a plan was hatched and St Joseph & The Helpers stepped in to provide €34,359 to extend and refurbish her home so that she could accommodate up to seventeen pilgrims.

This beautiful young widow thrives with her new found business and soon she was employing four people to help her in her 'pensione'. Her gratitude is deep and she never forgets how she was saved from poverty and distress. She welcomes all those who come to visit her and all those who come to stay with her and they in turn, the pilgrims to Medjugorje, bask in the warmth of her beautiful smile and warm hospitality, thanks to the generosity of St Joseph & The Helpers.

7. Supporting the Families

Since the inception of the charity, St Joseph & The Helpers has supported many poor families on a regular basis. In recent years, a Christmas donation of €1,500 is sent to Sr. Jelenka at the Kindergarten in Kiseljak so that she can help families in need with some extra money. Where there is a situation of alcohol abuse or domestic violence, Sr Jelenka buys the necessary food and household goods, instead of handing over the money whilst ensuring that no family goes without the very basic necessities.

In 2012 the Charity purchased a new apartment in Mostar for a family who were about to be evicted. The father had been imprisoned during the war and tortured. He has bullet wounds to his head and body which still cause him severe physical and psychological pain. He suffers from "Post-traumatic Stress Disorder" and cannot work, so the family struggle to survive on his €250 war invalid monthly pension.[8] The couple and their four children regularly turn to the Lord in prayerful thanks for all the gifts He has showered upon them through the goodness of friends and St Joseph & The Helpers charity.

In Easter, 2013, a father found solace in the knowledge that his family could be further helped by St. Joseph & The Helpers. His daughter, a young Political Science student had found a supportive donor through the kindness of Vesna Radisic in Medjugorje. Whilst on a visit to Vesna's house to re-unite with her sponsor and a director of the charity, to thank them for all the help which had been given to her and which they continued to give, the young lady's father seized the opportunity to ask for help with his house. He, his wife and

---

[8] **The family name** is withheld for reasons of confidentiality. However, as with all the families, these names are held in trust by St Joseph & The Helpers Charity. **Post-Traumatic Stress Disorder:** This is a psychiatric disorder characterised by an acute emotional response to a traumatic event or situation involving severe environmental stress, such as a natural disaster, aeroplane crash, serious automobile accident, military combat or physical torture .[Mosby's Medical, Nursing & Allied Health Dictionary, 6th edition (Mosby, USA, 2002) 1381].

seven children had come to Herzegovina from Bosnia after the war and had spent ten years living in a container house at Lubuskji refugee camp. To their delight, through the help of a German charity, they were offered a house in Hodovo, but unfortunately, the house was not insulated, resulting in being very hot in the summer and very cold in the winter.

On returning to Ireland, the kindly donor, who had already sponsored one young lady to undertake her nurse's training and continued to sponsor this man's daughter complete her Political Science course, found himself haunted by the father's face and his passionate plea, "can you help me with my house?". His heart was deeply moved and in response to the father's plea, he asked that when next the charity directors visited Medjugorje later that year in July, that they investigate the reality of the family's living conditions.

So in July 2013, two of the directors visited the family in Hodovo and what they found was that inspite of the family's great efforts to cover the windows and doors in order to keep their home cool, they stepped into a house that was stifling hot due to the high temperatures outside. In the winter, it was the opposite, and the family would brace themselves for the arrival of the "Bora", a fierce Adriatic wind which stretched its cold tentacles into the north facing wall of the house permeating into every crevice and destroying any warm air in its path.

After relating an emotional story of the plight of the family to their fellow pilgrims on their return to Medjugorje, another two people expressed to the directors, their desire to help. Estimates were soon gained from a local trusted builder and the house was totally insulated at a cost of €7,500. One man's kind heart served to open the hearts of others and in pooling the resources a wonderful gift was achieved for the family who had suffered so much.   Together, people can make a huge difference.[9]

[9] Support for any of the above causes can be given through :
St Joseph & The Helpers Charity, www.helperscharity.com or contact:
Pat Henry, Chairman (UK) at pat@helperscharity.com
Tel: +44 (0) 144239107 ; Mob: +44 (0) 7866224671 or
Donal O'Shea, Director (UK) at donal@helperscharity.com
Tel: +353 (0) 12858130;   Mob. +353 (0) 872500424.

Chapter IV

THE ELDERLY

Grandparents' Home, Vionica
St Luke's Home Care, Medjugorje.

1. The Grandparents' Home, Vionica

In the grounds of Vionica Orphanage, a few kilometres from Medjugorje, over thirty elderly people enjoy the peace and tranquillity of the beautiful "Grandparents' Home". The Home is a far cry from the poverty of the nearby refugee camp where many of them had previously been housed. There they lived in tin huts and had to queue for water, food and toilet facilities. St Joseph & the Helpers charity helped to build the Home on land given by Sr Kornelijie's family, cousins of the late Fr Slavko Barbaric who founded Mother's Village. Arthur McCluskey had recognised the importance of continuity from one generation to the next. The children of the Vionica Orphanage needed to know where their roots lay, for many had lost their parents and only some of the grandparents remained.

The two visitors, both nurses, gazed at the outside walls. It was difficult to tell that this was a home for the elderly. The eldest of the two stepped inside. She had trodden the corridors of many custom-built nursing homes in her professional life-time; but this was different. The window boxes were well kept; perhaps by the two old ladies who were leaning over one of the balconies, peering at the two strangers with curiosity. They waved and the nurses waved back, delighted at the instant welcome. Stepping inside the front door, they were met with a pristine marble floor, so clean and so polished, as

Cardinal Vinko Puljic and Arthur
– October 2007

Arthur, Fr Svetozar Kraljevic, Donal O'Shea,
"Night at the Dogs", Ireland, March 2008

Family Picture: Arthur, his mother and
six sisters, Ireland, 1987

Arthur, Sylvia (author), Fr Slavisa, Sr Lidija –
November 2010

Arthur and Fr Svet at St. Joseph Hall,
Mother's Village – May 2011

Pat Henry (Arthur's sister, Chairman UK), Susan Bond (Director UK),
Arthur, Fr Pero – Public Kitchen, Sarajevo – June 2011

The Grandparents' Home

Arthur and Danijela, the guide

Sister at the dining-room window
– May 2011

Chapel at Vionica Orphanage

From left to right taken at Dezevice: "Our Lady of the Snows", Cemetery, Jakov's Well

ARTHUR BY TIBOR DEVIC

Tibor never met Arthur but his pencil drawing captures his charisma and his infectious personality perfectly. Arthur's charity will sponsor this gifted young artist from Kiseljak through Art Academy and we welcome your help to establish an educational fund in Arthur's name.

Kindergarten at Bijele Polje – Arthur and Sr Marija – May 2011

Sr Dominika

Sr Jelenka

Arthur and Sr Janja – May 2011

Lisa, Fr Josip, Donal O'Shea at Visoko

well as an air of peace and tranquillity as the net curtains gently wafted in the warm afternoon breeze.

The little chapel to the right enticed the visitors to stop for a moment and reflect on the goodness of an omnipotent God. How much pain He must have felt as He witnessed the bewilderment and destruction of His aged souls, their deaths, their losses, fruits of the brutal war. They had spent their lives in their villages, raising their children, celebrating new births, kissing the hand held out with the cut finger, dancing at their weddings and then rocking their grandchildren in their arms. A life of quiet contentment, with ups and downs, hopes and disappointments, but overall a good life; and then, in their twilight years, tending to the children and the vegetables in the garden. What was it that prompted their neighbours to burn their houses, rape their daughters, murder their men? Too much pain, oh so much suffering, a life-time lost; a family destroyed, a neighbourhood gone and now every cell in their bodies haunted by the terrified screams of those last moments of their sons and daughters. How could they go on? They had nothing, nowhere to live, no food to eat, no life left to live and nothing, absolutely nothing left to give.

Arthur heard of their plight and of the plan to bring them closer to the children at the orphanages in Citluk and Vionica. What better task than giving their 'grandparent love' to the children who had no grandparents, no parents. Their aged physical disabilities could be a problem in moving around and the flashbacks continued to torture their very existence, but the children needed them; they needed to have someone to love and the old people needed someone to love them and love is not restricted to mobility. It is about time, about giving of oneself and these elderly grandparents had so much time, so much love to give.

The foundations were laid; the old lady in Ireland knew their plight. She understood the pain of old age, the weariness of a life-time of conflict and she gave; it was not much, but it was all she had, the widow's mite, and she knew it would make a difference. She had met Arthur and he had touched her heart with such gentleness, such honesty, such integrity: "Every penny goes straight to the project" he had told her, "the Directors pay for all the administration costs. Every cent goes to the people of Bosnia Herzegovina," he stressed.

The visiting nurses poked their heads into the kitchen; a baby slept quietly in a cot.   He was eight months old and had been abandoned by his young mother. The Sisters took care of him as they busied themselves over the pots of stew and vegetables. The nurses smiled at each other. A far distant scene from their own culture, but oh how tender and touching. The 'kitchen baby', they named him. He was so beautiful, so small, so content, sleeping soundly amongst the pots and pans. He felt safe, loved. He had nothing to fear now. The Sisters understood his loss; they too had been abandoned at the gates of the orphanage, but a life-time of love had persuaded them to give back to God what He had given to them. So they sung in praise and jubilation as they stirred the oatmeal in the mammoth pots, thanking God for the opportunity to care for this little one as they cared for the lonely, lost elderly souls upstairs.

Upstairs, Marija, Jelena and Katia, settled down to pray together. Their room was not luxurious but each had her own bed, her own little bed-side cabinet and, more importantly, they were together. They were not alone. An old hairbrush set sat eloquently upon a lace cloth, a small tin containing remnants of a past life, saved from the devastation and destruction. There were no photographs, no evidence of a family, friends, a loved one, a life; for that had all gone, but they were together and they sought comfort in each other. The nurses popped their heads round the door, "are we interrupting?" they asked.

"Come in" the old ladies beckoned with eager hands. The dialogue of smiles, hugs, kisses, touch, transcended all language barriers and exploded into laughter, offers of sweets, pride.

Along the corridor sat Ivan, no longer left in his old age to fend off the harsh north winds in a ramshackle hut. He had been confused, disorientated at first and sorrow his constant companion, particularly since his beloved wife, Marija, died shortly after coming to live at Vionica. His skin folded along his skeletal frame, but wrapped in a warm woolly jumper and thick purpose made trousers, he felt warm. He couldn't stand by himself and in the past, reaching out his arms in joy at the sight of Arthur took effort, but the toothless smile radiated into the nurses' hearts as they responded to his invitation to squeeze him tight.

The nurses moved on. Head at the foot of the bed, they noticed that one unplanned turn and she would fall on the floor. Experienced hands gently woke her, turned her round, tucked her in and kissed her tenderly. "Kiss me too" whispered the voice from the next bed. Pleading eyes, frail hands beckoned an immediate response. One nurse moved over quickly, exchanged greetings, one soul reaching out to another. "I am Lisa" the nurse said softly. "L-I-S-A" the old lady repeated, hesitatingly, wanting to please, desperate to belong. "Kiss me, Lisa" she pleaded. Lisa leant over and kissed her, held her hands for a while and stayed. What had those searching blue eyes seen? What had she experienced?

The garden brought healing; a little bench with chairs and shelter from the sun – PEACE. How the earth cried for peace. The children came from the orphanages, some with grapes freshly picked from the vines, others with sweets, some with ragged smiles, others with stories of life at school. But they came. No one was left out. They sat on the edge of the beds and with seriousness they related their problems, hurdles of youth to be overcome with understanding and a readily available ear listening intently.

One young man did not know that his grandmother had survived the war; his entire family had been destroyed in the conflict and he alone had survived being brought to the orphanage as a small infant. One day, he and the other young people from the orphanage walked to the Grandparents' Home to visit the old people. For a moment he thought it was his imagination as he stared at the newest resident in the home, but their eyes contacted and their spirits leapt in joy of recognition and grandmother and grandson rushed into each other's arms and held each other tight. They had found each other.

The History of the Grandparents' Home

At the same time as Mother's Village was being built, Sr Kornelijie and her sister, Sr. Josipa, were developing Vionica orphanage to accommodate children belonging to twenty-five families, where the parents had all been killed. Orphanages take time and money to build and initially their family handed over a hotel and some houses they owned in Medjugorje to provide shelter for the orphans. Little by little the orphanage was built and once the children moved there, the hotel and houses were used once again to accommodate pilgrims.

Shortly after St Joseph & The Helpers Charity was set up in 2004, Arthur McCluskey visited Sr Kornelijie (whom he knew from his days with the charity, 'Rebuild for Bosnia') as he wanted to sympathise with her on the death of her sister, Sr Josipa. He asked her if his new charity, St Joseph & the Helpers, could help in any way. Sr Kornelijie took him and his interpreter into the Chapel to pray. She then produced paperwork containing financial estimates on the building of the nursing home known as the 'Grandparents' Home'. The plan was to accommodate the surviving grandparents in the grounds of Vionica Orphanage but it had taken many years to get enough money to start building. €100,000 had been donated to Sr Kornelijie to build the Grandparents' Home. The shell was up but they had run out of funds. Arthur offered to enlist the help of his directors and find funding in Ireland and the UK for the project, recognising that the home would provide a safe haven for the older generation who had lost so much during the war in Yugoslavia. St Joseph & The Helpers raised the €90,000 required to help Sr Kornelijie Fr Kornelijie to complete the building which included €40,000 to install a lift.[1]

However, the Home has become more than just a haven; it is a witness to the tenacity and determination of a dignified generation of older people, to continue living. Many have lost everything and everyone in their family, living through the heartbreak of a shattered life and yet still they give of themselves to each other, to the children and to the foreign visitor, a living example of the depth of their faith, their uniqueness, their inner strength and love.[2]

2. St Luke's Home Care, Medjugorje.

Jane Dowd's little car, packed to the brim with nursing and medical provisions, trundled slowly, and cautiously, along a rugged dirt track There was nowhere for Jane to turn the car had she wished to do so and the stones scraped threateningly on the undercarriage of the little

---

[1] Initially, the old people were afraid to use the lift but that changed with time.
[2] This important work can be supported:
St Joseph & The Helpers Charity, www.helperscharity.com or contact:
Pat Henry, Chairman (UK) at pat@helperscharity.com
Tel: +44 (0) 144239107 ; Mob: +44 (0) 7866224671 or
Donal O'Shea, Director (UK) at donal@helperscharity.com
Tel: +353 (0) 12858130; Mob. +353 (0) 872500424.

Fiat. There was so much work to do, so many old people to tend to and sometimes it became impossible to visit everyone, but Jane and her nurses made every effort to ensure that every person had contact as often as possible.

Life had not always been like this for retired Irish nurse-educator Jane. Jane had a dream to work in Africa in her retirement but soon realised that God had other plans for her. She had come to Medjugorje many years previously and spent the greater part of a year assisting Sr Muriel provide life-saving provisions such as food and clothes, to those struggling to survive in remote areas beyond Medjugorje. When she first visited the outlying areas surrounding Medjugorje, she discovered many old, dying people without medical aid, life-saving drugs, food to eat, a stove for warmth and for those truly suffering and in pain, there was not even an Aspirin to relieve the ravages of cancer or dying. It had been a slow painful process. There were limited official organisations or agencies that she could rely on for help. Jane stepped out in faith, visiting those she knew were in need, providing the care, the medication, on the meagre contributions given to her from friends and relatives. She soon came to the realisation that her nursing skills, her years of experience, could be well used here in Bosnia and Herzegovina to help these fragile, sick, old people.

Jane and her nurses care passionately for their patients and her nurses are extremely grateful to have a steady job. As fully trained professional nurses they earn a third of what they would in the rest of Europe working for Jane's organisation, St Luke's Home Care, but nevertheless they are grateful for the job which recognises their skill and professional accreditation. Often these dedicated nurses are the only breadwinners in their family and without their wages they too would find it difficult to survive and support their children. Many of their trained colleagues cannot find work. Jobs are few for nurses in a health-care system inhibited by lack of the necessary funds to provide essential medical care. St. Luke's Home Care nurses are grateful for the opportunity to use their professional skills and talents and for the opportunity to care for their old people and support their struggling families.

Arthur first heard about Jane's work from one of the Directors who wanted to support Jane through St Joseph & The Helpers. When Arthur first met Jane, he identified immediately that the work she and her nurses were undertaking was an essential part of the provision of care in Bosnia and Herzegovina. Eager to help, he considered the suggestion to provide the wage for a nurse an excellent one and set about raising funds for that purpose. After two initial donations of €1,000, since 2010, St Joseph & The Helpers have given Jane €10,000 per annum and have an ongoing commitment to continue with this amount. This has enabled Jane to recruit a fourth nurse so they can reach the very neediest of her patients, many who, without her help, would have been abandoned to their fate, left to die in pain, or just left to die.

The little Fiat came to a stop outside an iron gate. Dressed in a headscarf, worn, dirty clothes, ragged boots, the old lady came to greet them. Her wrinkles belied her age of 70 years, for the harsh winters and the cold had battered her body adding 15 years to her malnourished skin. The sheer physical and psychological effort of keeping alive gnawed at her inflamed joints, resulting in knotted, debilitated hands and painful limbs. There had been three sisters originally, now there were two. The caring parish priest had built a new house for them on their land, to enable the three sisters to live out the rest of their lives in comfort; but on the day they moved, one sister died suddenly in the new house. The two remaining sisters were terrified; this new house was obviously "the dying house" and so they fled back to their hovel in a windowless steading without heating, refusing to return. Superstition and fear had won. The new house stood empty, sad and lonely in full sight of the two sisters who were content to retreat to the safety of their familiar home, curl into the heap of clothing on the battered bed which rested precariously on the dirt floor. To them the struggle against their harsh existence was tempered by the knowledge that they were alive and together. Each day they arose in the same clothes they had worn the day before and slept in that night. No one knew how long it had been since they had washed either themselves or the clothes. Coats became bedcovers and pillows, essential to keep them warm at night, but next day they would be worn to protect the women from the elements as they busied themselves with their daily chores around their land. Such was their existence.

Nearby the steading stood "the old house" where they had grown up together as children, housing some very starved and anxious looking hens which tried to peer through the filthy windows in curiosity at the sound of an approaching visitor. The sisters wanted someone to convert their old home so that they could live in it again, but this is a land where finance is scarce and to attempt such a project would be double the cost of their "new home" and out of reach financially for their kindly neighbours.

Their lives would be lived out in the old steading, packed full of litter and old clothes – clothes which at one time had adorned many good people including the nurses, but, in the sisters' debilitating state of mind, were misused, cast aside, their value unappreciated and the sacrifice of others unrealised. Poor mental health may have always been their companion. It was difficult to know, but it was obvious that the condition in which they lived only served to exacerbate their ability to function at any 'normal' level.

The wood stove gushed out yet another jet of toxic smoke. It had become an essential part of their lives, for without it they could not cook the carcases of the slaughtered chickens or the meat provided by the generosity of their neighbours. Without the old stove, the chances of them waking up on the cold winter mornings would have minimised, having succumbed to the claws of plummeting temperatures and hard frosts.

Patiently, the nurse took and monitored the sisters' blood pressures; one sister feigned faintness. The blood pressure was normal. Determined to grasp the attention of someone, she then feigned tears, but soon, just as quickly as they had appeared, they disappeared, as music blared from their old wireless and she decided to dance instead. There was little obvious reason to dance and sing and to the observer, her behaviour appeared puzzling, but her joy had increased and she became relaxed before moving onto her next inspired movement, that of inviting the nurses and visitors to join her in a prayer of thanksgiving.

Back into the car and time for reflection. What was the future for these two old sisters or for their next patients, the old couple living in similar conditions at the top of a steep pathway? Their house, at least, had windows, a warm stove and a decent settee where the old lady stretched out to receive care for her swollen legs covered in varicose ulcers; a result of her uncontrolled diabetes. The old man bent over, stirred the battered pot filled with stew, a mixture of whatever he could find in his small garden. It was difficult to say how old he was, but he took on the stature of someone in his late eighties. They had been married for many, many years and he would care for her to the very end, but memories flickered between them and tormented their feeble existence for they had lost almost everything and everyone in a ruthless war.

Perhaps that accounted for the piles of polythene bags stacked on every shelf, in every available space of every corner of the room. Full of what? No one really knew, but old newspapers, utensils, clothes, tinned food seemed to be the most predominant theme, in neat little bags, tied up with string for a time in the future. Insecurity dominated their lives, twisted their perception of daily living and shackled them to a past full of memories. They were content; they had each other, their faith and they were not left alone. They thanked God each day for the care that was given to them, the good fortune of the visiting nurses and they were grateful for the medication which kept them alive and free from pain.

Jane was aware that she did not have the resources needed for everyone, but she could visit and she could reach out to others; touching, holding, hugging and listening often became the most important part of her work, the medication needed for broken minds and lives. The old people knew that they mattered, that they were important and that they were not forgotten. Jane and her nurses 'told' them that, by their daily visits.

Some could not speak, impaired by loss of hearing or shrouded in shock. They never thought they would ever find themselves in these impoverished circumstances. These were a proud, dignified people. They knew that old age would be difficult, but many were still traumatised by what they had seen, heard and experienced in the Bosnian war. Some sat motionless, hands clasped in front of them, rocking quietly, or staring, just staring, eyes devoid of any emotion. There were few men left. A generation gone, both old and young mowed down, leaving only the women to bring forward a broken country. They have a quiet strength, these old people, but they were tired and Jane knew that without her nurses they may well have given up. So she ensures that they have wood for heating and cooking; she sources out good stoves for them to cook on and she strives to find food and clothes to care for them. She has no money to give them to pay the electricity bill, so sometimes they are without light, but she works hard to take the message of their plight to the government agencies that might be able to help and she prays each day that more help will come to these gentle people of the Balkans.

The nurses move on, and the smell of urine rushes out to greet the young nurse as she shouts "Kako ste, Eva?" ("How are you?").   It had always been like this: Eva, confined to bed, incontinent and totally dependent on the whim of an alcoholic nephew to bring her food. She was grateful for the visit, for she knew she would be washed, changed and cared for, that day and the next and in the days that followed. At 90 years old that was a blessing for which she thanked God throughout the day.

Eva knew also that the nurses would bring her bananas, biscuits and something warm to drink.   Sometimes that was all she had, but at least she had food, precious and nourishing, essential to keep her alive throughout the winter months, until the warmth of the summer sunbeams infiltrated her little room and gently touched her ancient cheeks. Eva was blind and her world was confined to a tiny bed, in the corner of a small room, with one small window to bring the outside world to her life.

In the summer, Eva loved to be taken out of her room to the porch so that she could sit in the old chair.   There she would listen to the sounds of the street, the chirping of the birds and the hub of life in the neighbourhood around her. But the outside also held danger for Eva for there were times when she became confused, often as a result of dehydration due to lack of provision and at these times Eva would be found crawling on her hands and knees on the road, into the pathway of oncoming cars. Gently, she would be helped back to her little house by those who found her, usually under the protection of her caring neighbours. Carefully, she would be tucked up in bed, reassured, kissed on the forehead and a small cool glass of water or hot tea would be held to her lips. Eva was one of the fortunate ones, living in a community who truly cared.

The nurses sat Eva up in bed and they washed her gently.   Due to their tender loving care Eva had no bed-sores, no red patches and her skin was soft and intact, free from the debilitating effects of urine saturates.   There are no washing facilities in the little cottage, so the urine soaked sheets and blankets are rinsed out in a small metal bucket of cold water and then hung on the porch railings to dry.   The smell of urine clings to the sheets but at least they are dry, and at least Eva can be assured of lying in a warm, dry bed each day, protected by incontinence pads.

At the weekends, sometimes Eva's niece comes to stay, sleeping in the little living-room adjoining the bedroom.   There is no connecting door, for both doors lead to the porch. Old photographs and treasured ornaments are frozen in time under the heavy blanket of dust that permeates the entire room, reflecting Eva's inability to care for her home, as well as a reminder that she too has memories, a past-life and a family. There, on the shelves, the trinkets will remain where they will continue to gather more dust, for although the kindness given to Eva from her niece includes feeding and caring for Eva at the weekend, there is no incentive or time to undertake the cleaning duties.   If no one comes at the weekend, Eva will lie in her urine soaked bed and pray, devoid of food, devoid of warmth, devoid of companionship, dependent on her kindly neighbour to bring her a warm drink, but who is too afraid to linger or come to the house if Eva's alcoholic nephew is in sight.   Sadly Eva passed away in 2012, but in the knowledge that in her twilight years, she was loved and cared for by Jane Dowd's nurses.

A call comes in and Jane listens to an urgent request to visit a woman dying of cancer.   She listens carefully, aware that she may be the only contact able to help this woman die peacefully in her own home. There is limited social service provision, no palliative care hospital and no government home-care nurse to give the pain-relieving medication; there is Jane and there are Jane's nurses, the nurses of St Luke's Home Care who will be the lifeline that is required to enable this woman to die with dignity. Her ethnicity is not important, her age is irrelevant, her religion is respected; what is important to the nurses of St Luke's Home Care is that each person is a living being, made in the image of God and should be accorded all the dignity and respect that comes with that gift. Jane Dowd and St Luke's Home Care need funding to carry out this work. They also need wheelchairs, walking frames, crutches, bandages, dressings, ointments, vitamins and other medicines, especially pain relief. Jane says "there is a deep longing in all of us to remain in our own homes to the end. How can mere words describe the privilege of assisting them on their final journey?"

Jane's nurses were unemployed before they were brought under the umbrella of St Luke's Home Care and there are many more nurses waiting for the opportunity to join the team, to provide such care. The spirit of dedication and commitment is given freely, but it takes money to pay for the provision of one nurse and all her equipment. Since 2009, St Joseph & The Helpers have contributed €37,000 to St Luke's Home Care. They continue to contribute €10,000 per year to cover expenses and enable Jane to buy equipment. At the time of writing, Jane and her nurses care for the sick, young and old people alike, across 53 villages. If Jane had more nurses to work with, more nurses to join her team, many more old people would be cared for in their own home, with the love, tenderness and compassion which is the hallmark of the nurses of St Luke's Home Care.[3]

---

[3] Jane Dowd and St. Luke's Homecare can be supported through:
St Joseph & The Helpers Charity, www.helperscharity.com or contact:
Pat Henry, Chairman (UK) at pat@helperscharity.com
Tel: +44 (0) 144239107 ; Mob: +44 (0) 7866224671 or
Donal O'Shea, Director (UK) at donal@helperscharity.com
Tel: +353 (0) 12858130;   Mob. +353 (0) 872500424.

Chapter V

REHABILITATION and RESPITE

Miracles Centre for Prosthetic Care, Potoci.
Respite Centre, Tomislavgrad.

1. The Miracles Centre for Prosthesis and Care: Potoci, Near Mostar

The word 'miracle' implies something extraordinary, supernatural, not really expected and perhaps that describes aptly what UK charity Miracles and its local Bosnia and Herzegovina non-profit partner 'Divita Miracles' are striving to do and "make it happen" for hundreds of physically and emotionally damaged men, women and children in Bosnia and Herzegovina.

It's not easy to watch another human being struggle to cope with the loss of a limb, but it is even more difficult to stifle the anger one feels at the loss of that limb due to a war. The 1992-1995 war caused the loss of an estimated 100,000 lives, displaced nearly half of the pre- war population of 4.4 million people and cost an estimated €100 billion in war damage.[1] The war turned Bosnia and Herzegovina from a medium income country to a poor one, and it is estimated that over half of its current population are poor or borderline poor and suffer serious shortage in all aspects of welfare.[2] Since 1996, over

---

[1] These figures have been taken from the Miracles Charity website. Please refer to www.miraclesthecharity.org for further information .
[2] Ibid.

1,660 people have been damaged by landmines and it is estimated that over 328 of these are children, 1 in 5 of every victim.[3]

Losing a limb in Bosnia and Herzegovina is not the same as losing a limb in the European Union or USA, where physical, psychological, spiritual, social and financial care is available to all who undertake rehabilitation. Losing a limb in Bosnia and Herzegovina means waiting, sometimes for ten or fifteen years until such time the "limb maker" can find the finances, the time and the material to make a new artificial limb to the required specification. The fractured, underfunded health-care system cannot provide the care that is required for these vulnerable people and many of the victims have not received appropriate medical treatment or prosthetic care. It also means being unemployed and since there is limited government support, somehow the broken man and woman must find a way to support his or her family or stand by helplessly and watch them suffer. The technicians are few, but this is the miracle; that they are there and they are making limbs.

The excitement of driving to the Miracles Clinic is culminated in heightened anticipation as one step is taken through the door; a beaming welcoming smile awaits, radiating warmth, and relief washes over the "beneficiary" like a thunderous waterfall as hope springs into action as he/she forges ahead through the modern corridors. The hall, the meeting place, echoes the intimate dialogue between amputee and staff and there is a feeling that someone is interested, really interested in the pain, suffering and humiliation which has accompanied the forgotten wounded and scarred soldier or civilian casualty these last few years. A triumphant sound of joy reverberates from the gymnasium, wrapping musically around the visitor's ears as a

---

[3] Ibid.

man takes his first shaky steps to freedom and independence. The muffled noise of a football bounces off the gymnasium wall as a triumphant body kicks the ball around with his newly fitted limb. Tears of joy trickle gently across the rugged facial curves of a gentle giant as he realises that NOW he can contribute fully to the village and family life. How many wounded souls are there, struggling for survival in Bosnia and Herzegovina with their broken bodies and minds?

The UK Charity "Miracles" joined forces with "Saint David's Relief (USA)". When Theo Ellert, the founder of 'Miracles' first visited Bosnia and Herzegovina on an aid mission in March 1993, she met up with Matthew Procter and they determined to commit long-term help in order to assist people re-build their lives.

In 2000, 'Miracles' launched an appeal to build its own specialist prosthesis centre where landmine victims can receive the ongoing treatment they so desperately need and by 1st May 2009, the 'Miracles Centre for Prosthesis and Care' was opened, funded by grants (which were the result of appeal letters) and private donations.

Initially, with just one Certified Prostheticist (CPO), Nihad Subasic, an average of one new limb a week was being made and fitted. Now, in 2013, there is one CPO and one assistant/trainee prostheticist and their aim is to continue to make one new limb a week and assist in as many corrections as possible. It is unclear how many people are in immediate need; three years ago, the figures ran at about approximately 1,650 people based on amputees not having had a new limb update for over five years, hence the need for corrections. It is a slow process; the work, so urgent and necessary is hampered by the lack of funds (there is limited government aid) and the high cost of materials and components. Children need their prosthetics altered or remade at least once a year, sometimes twice a year to accommodate for growth. Without this regular support their prosthetic limbs are useless. If there were more technicians and more funding then more could be done to address the waiting list. Perseverance has enabled the work to grow.

A Response to Prayers:
A chance encounter and a meeting with Arthur McCluskey resulted in funding from St. Joseph's & The Helpers not only for limbs, but also for funding holidays for the children in the home in Zenica 'Dom I Porodica'."

A short spiritual exercise:
Mathew reflects, "We are encouraged to pray; Saint Paul says 'pray without ceasing.' Saint Ignatius of Lloyola, founder of the Jesuit Order invites us to really open up our imagination, that is to say, imagine yourself in a given situation, e.g., a scene in the Gospel, a landmine victim, a child living in a state run home for disadvantaged, what it is like to be displaced or homeless.

Consider this, an imaginary letter to Arthur:

Dear Arthur,

If only you could see the children this summer; they have grown so much since you first met them and soon, very soon, they will be thinking of so many other things – stepping out into the world, education if possible, work, definitely, if available. These seaside holidays were the best time in their lives, a time when they ran free on

97

*the beach, unrestrained from the shackles of non-
identity, lost in the moment of pure joy, forgetting
for a time that they had no family, no
grandparents, no parents, but just for one week,
an ordinary, normal, child, like all the thousands
of other children throughout the world.*

*Oh Arthur, if only you could see the benefits, how
love takes many forms, but in this case, how the
benefactors have given these children a gift, so
precious, it will remain in their hearts forever.*

*Thank you dear Arthur for bringing all these
beautiful people into our lives."*

For Matthew, Arthur is 'a man bearing fruit'. Outside the
Centre, Mathew points to the little fig tree which he has planted
in Arthur's name. The land is dry (it is summer) a tiny shoot
of green, leaning in the direction of the hills behind, a beautiful
land but filled with mines from the war. "No one knows where
they are", Mathew reflects quietly, "One wrong foot, and
'pouffff' it is all over – a lost limb, a lost life. There were no
maps showing exactly where the mines were laid and there are
over half a million landmines unaccounted for", he explains.
"That means that they could be lying waiting quietly in the
earth, ready to explode at a moment's touch".

Many have lost their limbs and the war has disfigured many
men, women and children. So many innocent children have
laughingly kicked a football, stepped onto a mine and have
been catapulted into an agonizing haze of pain, shock, near
death and permanent disability; a life-time of trauma, if they
survived. So many traumatized little children are walking

around, at first with no bandages, no walking-aids, no antibiotics; then infection sets in, necessitating further amputation and further agony. Most of the children have to wait ten years or more for the chance of a prosthesis, being deprived of a normal childhood and the pleasures that should bring.

Since 2009, St Joseph & The Helpers have funded limbs for over seven people. One of them was Jakov, a father of three who lost his leg when he stepped on a landmine. His new leg has changed his life dramatically, enabling him to drive a car and earn some money for his family.[4] Azra was nineteen years old when she lost her left leg to cancer; "the worst day of her life," she reminisces. This tragic situation meant that she could no longer continue to train as a hairdresser. Azra was at the Centre for a fitting when Matthew introduced Arthur and some of the directors to her, explaining later that she was finding it difficult to support herself financially. Arthur was moved by this courageous young lady and the directors agreed to provide the necessary financial support to enable her to continue High School. She is now studying Social Work at University at a cost to the Charity of €2,600 per year. She has cast aside her crutches and learnt to walk for a second time. A new limb was life-changing for Azra and it has enabled her to regain a level of normality.

With so few technicians and restricted funds, it will take years for all of those people waiting to be given the chance to start again - which they deserve. The generosity of so many people including the directors and donors of St Joseph & The Helpers makes it possible for this work to continue one at a time. The clinic could help more if there were more technicians and more resources; it all centers on available funds.

---

[4] Surname withheld for reasons of confidentiality.

One of 'Miracles' objectives are to train two local citizens as Certified Prostheticists (CPOs) to an internationally recognized qualification. This will enable other men and women to be trained 'in-house' as prostheticists and in doing so, activity in the centre would increase and the most vulnerable of the people, the children, could be given that necessary prosthetic care at an early stage.

In addition, there is a great need to develop a community based rehabilitation program in the centre for all landmine victims, which can offer much needed psychosocial community support. It is not just a matter of losing a limb and coping with the physical disability; it is about treating the whole person, physically, psychologically, socially and spiritually, in order for that person to heal and grow. This would in turn increase the numbers of staff in the centre, thus providing essential jobs, which are much needed in the local community.[5]

2. TOMISLAVGRAD – Respite Centre for Children with Special Needs

To the north-east of Split in Croatia, approximately 65 kilometres as the crow flies lies the municipality of Tomislavgrad in Bosnia and Herzegovina. The city of Tomislavgrad is an ancient city going back to 4,000 BC and its foundations are built on rich culture, history and archaeological interests. In the municipality there are approximately 26,000 residents, the majority of whom are Croats, much reduced from the pre-war population of more than 30,000 people. The poor

---

[5] In 2012 and 2013, St Joseph & The Helpers committed €10,000 to Miracles Charity to be used for prosthetic care and hope to do so annually.

economic situation during and after the 1992-1995 war saw many of the population migrate to Germany, Australia and other parts of Croatia and they have not returned.

There is some industry in Tomislavgrad, mainly associated with transport and construction. There is hotel accommodation and café-bars, but on the whole, like most cities in Bosnia and Herzegovina, there is over 40% unemployment and this leads to the most essential of services being underfunded. In this climate, it is difficult to perceive how the most vulnerable of society can ever be given an opportunity to thrive. What do you do for the child and young adult who has Special Needs and who has limited prospect of specialist care and little hope for the future? What do you do for the parents, the devoted carers of these vulnerable members of society, who care for them diligently with tenderness, faithfulness and love, twenty-four hours a day, seven days per week? What can you do for them in a country which has little resources, a fragmented health-care system, and limited governmental support?

There are many different aspects of Special Needs; there is the child or the young adult with behavioural or psychological disorders, or perhaps there is the child who was born into a loving family but has genetic disorders, intellectual disabilities and the inability to undertake a normal learning process. Many of the children or young adults pinned with the label of "Special Needs" just need assistance for disabilities that could be mental, or psychological, or physical, or even social. Some may need support with Down's syndrome or blindness, cerebral palsy, cancer, diabetes, a physical need; but others may have different problems such as autistic disorder, a psychological and developmental need. All the children and young adults are special, and all of them have something special outwith the norm which needs support, so that each one reaches his or her full potential. It is exhausting work for the family; one which drains the family's energy and strength and they too need support to re-energise, refresh, re-vitalize.

Sr Dominika (from Kiseljak and then Bijelo Polje) was born in Tomislavgrad and she knows the desperation the people feel in finding a way to provide services for children and young people with Special Needs. It is a subject close to her heart as her own sister's husband is blind, their son is autistic and their little girl has since been born blind.[6] The little girl has had cataract operations and now has 5% vision.

In October 2011, Donal O'Shea, Director of St Joseph & The Helpers, accompanied by Christy and Rose Carolan, responded to Sr Dominika's request by visiting Tomislavgrad and it was there that the Mayor, Ivan Vukadin, accompanied the visitors to view the premises used at that time. The conditions were terrible and totally unsuitable; the centre was housed in an old building with many stairs and many obstacles. At that time, they could only cater for eleven children, a drop in the ocean in relation to the numbers of children and young adults with Special Needs who required care.

During that visit, the Mayor asked for help to complete a School/Respite Centre for children and young adults with Special Needs. The shell of the new building was up but work ceased in 2011 due to lack of funds. The total project cost was €441,000 and Tomislavgrad municipality had spent on the

---

[6]**Autistic disorder**: "a pervasive developmental disorder with onset in infancy or childhood, characterised by impaired social interaction, impaired communication and a remarkably restricted repertoire of activities and interests [Mosby's Medical, Nursing & Allied Health Dictionary, 6th ed. (2002) 162].

project the €170,000 donation which they received from the Croatian Government plus €50,000 from various sources. When St Joseph & The Helpers charity became involved, €221,000 was outstanding to complete the project. With the promise of financial help from the charity, the building work re-started and soon, thanks to the generosity of donors, the charity donated €190,000. At that time in 2012, €31,000 remained outstanding to reimburse fully the builder who had completed the work but showed such faith in the Mayor, Mr Ivan Vukadin, in the promise of funds from The Helpers in Aberdeen, Scotland and in St Joseph & The Helpers charity, knowing that he would receive full payment.

In September 2012, a first Charity Ball was organised in Aberdeen, Scotland on behalf of St Joseph & The Helpers with the intention of raising funds for the charity and promoting the needs of the Respite Centre in Tomislavgrad.[7] Ivan Vukadin, Mayor of Tomislavgrad, accompanied by his wife Veronika and his cousin Vinko as interpreter, travelled from Tomislavgrad to attend the Ball. All their expenses were paid but Ivan Vukadin ensured that the financial cost was minimal; he and his wife travelled a lengthy journey by car from Tomislavgrad to Graz in Austria, where Vinko lives, before flying from Austria to the United Kingdom.

Ivan Vukadin is a good Mayor, a builder of schools, who works very hard to attract business into his diminished area. He has been voted 'Best Mayor' in Bosnia and Herzegovina and is

---

[7] The charity is indebted to the work and organisation of the two Charity Balls in September 2012 and September 2013 by Lynn Newborn, Mark Wilson, Jenny Allan and Steve and Toni Brady. All are connected with the Oil Business in Aberdeen and worked tirelessly to encourage their colleagues in the industry to attend the Balls in order to raise much needed funds for the charity and for the completion of the Respite Centre in Tomislavgrad.

well respected which is evidenced by the fact that the contractors finished the work and were prepared to wait for payment. He is totally committed to raising the necessary funds for the ongoing work in the centre which will help the people of Tomislavgrad. Ivan was repeatedly told the Centre could not be built; it could not happen. With faith he persevered and, through Sr Dominika, found a way to Arthur's charity, St Joseph & The Helpers. Another connection led to his meeting with Marisa Maragno and Paolo Freisinger who in time offered to fully furnish and equip the School and Respite Centre. Marisa and Paolo live in Padova (Padua) Italy, where there is a School for over 800 children and young people with Special Needs. They were instrumental in organising the staff from the Tomislavgrad project to visit Padua to study how things are managed there. In time, staff from Tomislavgrad will work and train for short periods in Padua and vice versa.

On July 8th, 2013, the Respite Centre was officially opened at Kovaci, Tomislavgrad. It was attended by two directors of St Joseph & The Helpers Charity who felt enormously proud to be a part of such a wonderful development. Marisa and Paolo were also in attendance and all the visitors had a translator alongside so they could understand what was being said. Young girls dressed in bright red cheer leader costumes stood either side of a red carpet in front of the entrance to the brand new building. One of those girls was the daughter of Ivan and Veronika Vukadin. Ivan gave a short speech in which he thanked the donors who made this dream come true. The Centre is the first of its kind in Western Herzegovina. The local county will fund the salaries while the Tomislavgrad Municipality will cover all other costs including transport of the children to and from the School.

Ivan thanked the people of Ireland and the United Kingdom who helped to fund the Centre and he thanked the people of Scotland very especially for their hospitality in September 2012. He also thanked Marisa and Paolo for their amazing support and generosity in providing furniture and equipment for the building. Stipe Curtic, a blind man and father of two children who will use the Centre, responded on behalf of the parents. He had written a song which was played at the Opening Ceremony in which he describes the Centre as a gift from heaven. The building, which is called Nova Nada (New Hope), was blessed by Fr Gabriel Mioc, a local Franciscan priest and then people walked through the building, amazed at what they saw. It is built in the style of an Austrian Chalet in keeping with the previous building on the site and is far more spacious than one would expect from the outside. Many parents of the children and young people with Special Needs approached the directors to say thank you from their hearts – the language of love and gratitude needed no translation.

How will this new building help these special children and young adults with Special Needs? First there is a building, uniquely built, thoughtfully designed to house the services required for these special people. Second, there is a place, a 'home from home' where this group can go, to spend some time in respite from the family and give the family themselves respite. Then there are the opportunities: the opportunity for the therapists, parents and 'clients' to set goals and monitor progress in a dynamic environment, one which provides support and understanding on the needs of all concerned in the family. Instead of focusing on what the individual cannot do, a negative approach, there is a focus on what the person CAN do, a positive approach. Often, discovery is encountered as a new strength is found in the individual; a hidden talent waiting to be brought to the fore, a triumph, a realisation that a new challenge is being met and conquered.

Then there is the support network, a comfort that other families are travelling the same journey and encountering similar difficulties. A time to meet, share a coffee and warmly baked bread, to unburden the load, gain new information and new ideas, and laugh, the most important of all; the healing power of laughter and companionship. This is especially important where children and young adults have conditions that require ongoing treatment, frequent tests, and hospitalisation. A roller-coaster of emotions arises in child or young adult as well as their parents and wider family. Hopes realised and then smashed; pain and suffering to be dealt with, equipment which is so readily available in other parts of Europe, to be found, if at all available. Frustration, anger, sadness, despair, then relief, excitement, laughter, happiness, daily visitors in an unending cycle of caring.

On top of that there are the difficulties of dealing with a child or young adult with behavioural problems, due to an undiagnosed or chronic physical, psychological or social problem. Coping strategies need to be developed in order for the family to cope with the uncertainty of behavioural change. Without these strategies, the wider family can fall into disarray and this may add new psychological problems to any member of the family.

The children themselves must be given the opportunity to learn, to develop and so educators are required with specialisms that will meet the needs of the blind child, the deaf child, the child who cannot speak, the child who has difficulty in learning. The employment of these special teachers opens a new world to the vulnerable person with special learning needs and there is pride in the success of gaining one small step each day to a new found understanding. In turn, an adult, trained specifically for this purpose, is given the opportunity to work, to pass on his/her knowledge and skills and to be paid for doing so. In an area of great unemployment, this is a chance of a life-time: the opportunity to provide for one's family whilst bringing light and life into the person with Special Needs.

Toys are needed in the centre; books, drawing materials, crayons, paint, special equipment to encourage walking, writing, special educational tools, specialised bikes to mobilise and so much more: curtains for the windows to frame the sunshine and the snow, carpet for the sleeping room which houses the little cots and beds, bright coloured utensils to encourage eating – the list is endless, for this is a home, not just a specialist area, it is a home for families who need specialist care and love. [8]

Nova Nada, New Hope, the School/Respite Centre at Tomislavgrad, is well named as it has become a symbol of hope for the directors of St Joseph & The Helpers Charity. It is the first building project taken on since Arthur's death in August 2011. He never knew of its existence but the directors feel sure that he would greatly approve. It fits with the charity's mission statement: "we aim to relieve poverty and advance education." The Centre will provide jobs for 8 – 10 specialists and also provide jobs for many ancillary staff. This project is testimony

---

[8] If you would like to help Mayor Ivan Vukadin with this new and worthwhile project, please contribute through:
St Joseph & The Helpers Charity, www.helperscharity.com or contact:
Pat Henry, Chairman (UK) at pat@helperscharity.com
Tel: +44 (0) 144239107 ; Mob: +44 (0) 7866224671 or
Donal O'Shea, Director (UK) at donal@helperscharity.com
Tel: +353 (0) 12858130; Mob. +353 (0) 872500424.

that the charity is alive and thriving and that it continues to build on Arthur's deep, strong foundations. However, just as in Arthur's lifetime, none of this would be possible without fundraising by other people and donations from the charity's generous and loving donors.

Chapter VI

THE HUNGRY

Pastoral Centre and Public Kitchen, Dobrinja, Sarajevo

The steps to the abandoned "Nuclear Fallout Bunker" in the small suburb of Dobrinja, are strewn with litter, abandoned, no longer scrubbed clean but once constituted the umbilical cord of survival, the link to the mother who would feed and sustain both body and soul. Pushing aside the debris, the visitor is grateful that the hungry citizen no longer has to enter these gates of a post communist era. Instead he can turn to the sparkling new public kitchen nearby, to be met with a modern, chaotic but friendly Fr Pero or one of his many helpers.

Dobrinja, the site of the 1984 Olympic Village, is known for its capacity to survive, to stem the tides of starvation. In January 1993, with pick-axe and shovel, the first bucketful of debris was removed from what would become known as "The Sarajevo Tunnel."[1] The Siege of Sarajevo began early in 1992 and lasted until 29th February 1996 – the longest siege of any capital in the history of modern warfare. According to general information, it lasted three times longer than the Siege of Stalingrad and one year longer than the Siege of Leningrad. 11,000 civilians were killed or went missing, over 1,500 of them children.[2] An additional 56,000 were wounded, including

---

[1] www.en.wikipedia.org/wiki/Sarajevo_Tunnel
[2] http://en.wikipedia.org/wiki/Siege_of_Sarajevo;
http://www.bbc.co.uk/news/world-europe-17617775

almost 15,000 children. The people lived in constant fear of death. A plan to build the Sarajevo Tunnel was their salvation.

Within four months, 1,500 metres had been completed successfully, linking two neighbourhoods, Dobrinja (which was under siege on one side of the airport), with the neighbourhood of Butmer on the free side, allowing food, humanitarian aid and war supplies to the starving population of 30,000 people in their high-rise buildings. Dobrinja has become synonymous with compassion and fortitude for it has withstood first the massacres of June 1, 1993, when two mortars fell on 200 people on a football pitch, where a make-shift game of football had been set up by local children; and then again, it is said, when there was no food left, the population had been forced to eat grass from the nearby park in order to survive.

There is a little chapel in the nuclear bunker, for there is little use in providing food for the mere body if the soul was starving and dying.   When it was in use, Fr. Pero would give thanks to God for the provision of the food, stacked at random in the humidity of the store next to the chapel.   Room was scarce and there was no other corner where these precious nutrients could be stored, and so cabbages, carrots and turnips were piled on top of each other in an airless room devoid of light.   This was a life-line, the source of sustenance and nutrition for body and soul, ready for the pot to feed the 250 desolate men, women and children who found their way to the nuclear bunker on a daily basis, clutching their "passport" from Social Services.

There are many hungry and poor people in the city of Sarajevo, but to qualify for a meal from "Kruh St. Ante" (the Bread of St. Anthony), a Franciscan charity operating from the beginning of the 1992-1995 war, one needs a certificate from the Department of Social Work.   Without that precious "passport" one should be turned away, but in reality it would be hard to deny the person bread to eat, for a mere certificate.

As now, meals were cooked in the kitchen from Monday to Friday, to be consumed at the few little tables or at home, or sitting on the grass verge nearby or just standing near the bunker; too precious to risk being snatched away by the starving neighbour or stray dog. Meals for Saturday and Sunday were given out on Friday; the dedicated cooks immersed in a hive of accelerated activity preparing 750 'meals' to ensure the provision of a satisfying, non-hungry weekend.

The time had come: a new parish in Sarajevo, Dobrinja parish, had been entrusted to the Franciscan Order. A site had been identified, ready to hold the new church which would form a triangle with a nearby Serbian Church and a Muslim Mosque. Fr Pero would move from his old abode to the new building, so the plan would be to build first the Pastoral Centre which would provide a home for Fr Pero but also would house a public kitchen where meals for the 250 people would continue to be provided. Since this is only one of two kitchens feeding the poor in Sarajevo, it was essential that the work continued unhindered, in the transfer from nuclear bunker to pastoral centre.

In the new plans, a nuclear bunker must also be provided, a legal requirement in Bosnia and Herzegovina, otherwise the parish would have to pay a hefty sum to avail of government facilities. Tucked underneath the pastoral centre, a new nuclear bunker is built and for the time being, until such time when funds are raised to build a separate church, this is now the place of worship. It has its own beauty: flowers adorn the front of the altar, laid with care and gratitude by an elderly lady whose hand and forearm were blown off by an explosive during the "Siege of Sarajevo".[3] The statues of St Frances and St Anthony watch tenderly over the little flock who faithfully kneel in prayer, each with his own way of communicating with a beneficent God.

There is a new store for the vegetables and meat, cool, spacious, airy and with a little light even though it lies in the basement; a perfect place to stem the invasion of any unwanted microbes or mammals. The cabbages gleam in the coolness of the air, crisp and pristine, waiting to be taken on their journey to feed the hungry families of Dobrinja. The meat is protected from the warm air hovering in the corridors above by a cool ventilated bunker.

There is a conference room to be used for educating the young priests and to be utilised by the local community. Fr Pero proudly shows off his new office, inviting the imagination to look beyond the cement floors and unbuilt walls. He points out where his chair will stand, his desk and shelves for his books. He beckons to the corridor to show where the vestments will hang in the newly built cupboard, still as yet on the drawing board, but with faith, he knows that God, through the generosity of others, will provide the much needed furniture for the rooms.

The foundation for both buildings, pastoral centre and church, had been laid and the shell of the pastoral centre had emerged and was standing, but then the money ran out. By June 2011, €350,000 had been spent, but the parish owed €50,000 of that money and so the building work ceased, whilst they tried to

---

[3]The "Siege of Sarajevo" lasted three years from 1992-1995.
www.en.wikipedia.org/wiki/Siege_of_Sarajevo

find the money to buy the materials and pay the labourers for their much needed skills. Some of their money had come from sources outwith the country, but promises had been broken and some had abandoned Fr Pero without explanation.

Money is tight in Bosnia and Herzegovina and in early June 2011, just two months prior to Arthur's death, Fr Pero and Cardinal Vinko Puljic wrote to St Joseph & The Helpers asking for support.

 The letter arrived with the accompanying trumpet of an official stamp, but underneath the officialdom lay a plea for help to support and finance this much needed project:[4]

---

[4] Printed with the permission of, Pat Henry, Chairman, St. Joseph & The Helpers Charity (U.K.) and Donal O'Shea, Director, St. Joseph & The Helpers Charity (UK) who was Director of St. Joseph & The Helpers Charity in Ireland at that time.

ŽUPA SVETOG FRANJE ASIŠKOG –DOBRINJA,Sarajevo

Trg Djece Dobrinje 1
BiH 71000nSarajevo
E mail: pero.karajica@gmail.com
UniCreditBank
Bank Account: 20013471101
IBAN:BA393386904830099304
SWIFT:UNCRBA 22

fra Pero Karajica
Franjevačka Teologija
Aleja Bosne Srebrene 111
Mobilni:0038765582033

Bi. 36/2011.

ST.JOSEPH AND THE HELPERS
CHARITY LTD
P.O. Box 10486
DUBLIN 18 IRELAND

Subject: **Petition for help in the construction** of Parish Church and Parish House in Dobrinja, Sarajevo

Dear Sir,

On behalf of our Parish Community and Pastoral Council I would like in this way to thank all well-meaning people and institutions for everything they have done for the beginning of the construction the **pastoral centre of St. Francis of Assissi in Dobrinja.** The new parish has been entrusted to us Franciscans for the needs of the Catholics and of all well-meaning fellow-citizens. Many hungry and poor people have been for several years fed in the public kitchen of St. Anthony's Bread that has been active since the beginning of the war. The city of Sarajevo is a good example of coexistence and cooperation with other churches and faiths. The construction-works are done by the company GRADNJA from Kiseljak with which we have signed a contract on 29. 9. 2010. in amount of **1.075.746,77 KM.** We started with the construction-works on 15. 10. 2010. and reckon to finish roof-construction and basic plumbing and electrical installations by the end of 2011.

We build the church with the help of our parishioners and other benefactors and institutions in Bosnia and in the world. On 1. 2. 2011. we continued with the construction of the pastoral centre in Dobrinja that could last **approximately 3 years.** The works are getting on well, and recently we were visited and encouraged by the cardinal Vinko Puljić. It should be mentioned that within the parish house we build **public kitchen** of St. Anthony's Bread where will be fed the citizens in need living in the area of Dobrinja, **approximately 250 persons per day.**

In this way **we would like to ask you to help us** according to your possibilities in order to be able to continue with the construction on behalf of all well-intentioned people and our parishioners.

I would like to thank you most cordially for your understanding and support and pray for God's blessing and the intercession of st. Francis for you and your collaborators. I greet you with franciscan greeting PEACE AND GOOD!

Sarajevo, 21.3.2011.

Fra Petar Karajica, parish priest

I recommend this project from my heart!
With cordial greetings!

Vinko Cardinal Puljic, Archbishop

115

In June 2011, Arthur, Pat and Susie (two UK directors) visited the project. Arthur wanted to help and hoped that in time the charity might find sponsorship for the provision of meals. After Arthur's death, €180,250 was sent to Fr Pero so that he could complete the much needed kitchen. Over €30,000 of that money was raised by the hard-working committee who organised the Aberdeen Charity Ball in June 2012.[5]

It is difficult to imagine the plight of the hungry and only experience can bring that understanding and empathy. However, without reservation, through the generosity of those whom God had touched to share with those without, the realization of a dream came to pass.

Opening of Public Kitchen

On 2nd October 2012, excitement bubbled from the kitchen of the Pastoral Centre as busy staff and helpers prepared for the official opening ceremony. It was a wonderful day; a day of great joy and celebration that at last something positive had been achieved through the generosity of so many good people. In the presence of representatives of "The Bread of St. Anthony" and donors from Ireland and the UK, Fr Lovro Gavran, Provincial of the Franciscan Province of Bosna Srebrena, undertook the solemn task of blessing the kitchen.

---

[5] The charity is indebted to the work and organisation of the Ball in 2012 by Lynn Newborn, Mark Wilson, Jenny Allan and Steve and Toni Brady. All are connected with the Oil Business in Aberdeen and worked tirelessly to encourage their colleagues in the industry to attend the Ball in 2012, in order to raise much needed funds which contributed to the Pastoral Centre.

He said,

"In the area of Dobrinja this kitchen has operated from the war days, when people of good-will tried to save the lives of a starving population. After the war, the kitchen worked in a war shelter. This is one of three kitchens of "The Bread St. Anthony", two are in Sarajevo and one in Vares; over 1,000 meals are delivered daily.

In the Dobrinja centre around 300 meals will be prepared and served for the poor people, along with a certain number for those who will get a meal at their home because they are disabled or seriously ill.

Our friends from St Joseph & The Helpers gave the funds for the construction of this kitchen and for that we are sincerely grateful. We strive to help all people who are in need, especially those who are hungry. Unfortunately the unemployment rate in Bosnia and Herzegovina is very high; there are a lot of hungry people. That's why we want to provide at least one meal a day, but not from our reserves, because we do not have any, but through beneficiaries. Everyone's help is welcomed.

The 'Bread of St. Anthony' organisation is feeding the poor of all nationalities and their number is growing from day to day. Serbs, Croats, and Muslims are coming for food, and there are no differences between people in need, no matter who they are. Users will be able to eat at the centre or take food home or food will be delivered for those who are not able to come to the centre. This new centre will ease the distribution of meals for the staff who prepare and distribute the food.

May God give new hope to these people through the good deeds of good people and may He bring hope and happiness to the poorest among us, who need our help the most".[6]

---

[6]Fr Pero needs funds to support the ongoing building of the Centre and Church. If you wish to contribute, please do so thrugh:
St Joseph & The Helpers Charity, www.helperscharity.com or contact:
Pat Henry, Chairman (UK) at pat@helperscharity.com
Tel: +44 (0) 144239107 ; Mob: +44 (0) 7866224671 or
Donal O'Shea, Director (UK) at donal@helperscharity.com
Tel: +353 (0) 12858130;   Mob. +353 (0) 872500424.

Chapter VII

THE YOUTH: THE FUTURE OF BOSNIA AND HERZEGOVINA

Education: A broad and dynamic vision

The preliminary exams in the rambling old school in a tiny part of Scotland rumbled on without too much incidence except the usual moans, complaints, post-mortems of difficult papers which tumbled from the weary shoulders of the fourth form pupils. In a few years time, the burden would seem light as they shifted from the "care-free" days of school and on to college and university. Some would leave school altogether, find a job or a trade that would put them in good stead for an off-shore job in the oil industry. It was expected: a job, college, university, it was there for all, free education in Scotland: no financial worries, a given and expected rite of passage to adulthood.

Not so for Tijana in Mostar. She wanted desperately to be a teacher, but that meant her refugee parents had to choose between provisions for the rest of the family and providing her with an education. Not only the fees, but books, bus fares, clothing; all had to be considered. How could one child in a family of six children take all the spoils? The worried frown on her father's brow tormented her and her precious mother, so thin, so proud of her talented daughter, haunted her. Tijana knew what a struggle this would be for her family and she could not put them through this torment. She had made the decision; she would have to refuse the place in college to train as a teacher and she would work, find a job if at all possible, in order to help her family. She had no right to expect an education when her own siblings had to sacrifice everything. One day she would follow her dream, but not now, not at this time; it would have to wait.

It was difficult to stand by and watch such a talented young lady turn her back on an opportunity. St Joseph & The Helpers had already provided four new computers for the Hostel run by the 'School Sisters of St. Francis in Mostar', which accommodates students to the colleges in Mostar; but what use were computers if there were no talented students to operate them? Donal O'Shea, a Director of the charity heard of Tijana's plight and sprung into action. Without hesitation, it was agreed to support this talented young lady through college.

Arthur had dreamed of providing bursaries to support young people through college. How else could this magnificent country ever hope to re-establish itself in the world if its young were not given the opportunity to be educated? This was only one example and only the future would reveal the fruits of this generous action, as in turn Tijana would foster and form the inquisitive minds of the next generation. Without education, without help to support the young of Bosnia and Herzegovina, there is no future and that is why St Joseph & The Helpers reaches out to individuals to help them achieve that much needed education and in turn ensures an educated, liberated country of the future. St Joseph & The Helpers sees Education as the key to freedom and development.

Further to the north of Mostar, two dynamic educational systems are thriving; one, an institution of classical education and seminary training and the other a new vision incorporating spiritual, social, formal education to meet the needs of a new generation of Bosnia and Herzegovina's young people. Both are essential for the long term development of the country and both are grounded in their experiences of the past and hope for the future.

1. Visoko: Franciscan Secondary School and Seminary

Florence walked through Visoko for the last time. She had met Arthur McCluskey the year before and at that time walked through the corridors of the Franciscan Secondary School with enthusiasm, showing to her visitors the hidden gems of the newly refurbished school. But now it was June 2011 and after seven years of loving Bosnia, the young American knew it was time to say goodbye. She was weary; she felt tired and the once great challenge of assisting the Franciscan Priests at the School had become stifling. One minute she felt that she would not last another second there and another she felt like crying, not just because she was going, but because she felt that Bosnia was sad; not just sad, but tragic. Maybe that was what drew her to it; she knew that if you can't face pain and ease it, you never will grow as a person. As she walked, she reflected on what she had learnt; she was 29 years old now and many of her generation had moved on with their lives, gaining degrees, important career positions, marrying and having children; now she was starting over in her life even though she was constantly being asked when she would return.

The Franciscan priests did not want her to leave; they were praying for that intention, knowing that it would take a very special person to replace this young American who spoke fluently in the Slavic language. They too had suffered much in their time. They had struggled to keep their school viable, the only classics program secondary school in Bosnia and Herzegovina. The educational institution itself had been established in Kreševo in 1882 and after a move to Guča Gora close to Travnik, the school moved in 1900 into the then newly constructed facility in Visoko.[1] It was one of the most prestigious educational institutions in Bosnia and Herzegovina open to all religious groups and in the academic year 1939-1940 it had 536 students: 156 seminarians, 213 students from the local area and 167 boarders.

Fr Josip reflected on the years; it had not been easy even though from the very beginning the Franciscan Seminary School had been connected to the Franciscan Classics-programme Secondary School and open to all hard working students of all faiths, without discrimination. It was the Franciscan tradition to teach the classics: The Arts, Latin, Greek amongst other subjects. Many people from town wanted to attend their school to receive a good education and that is why they decided to develop a new building for students who did not want to become Franciscans but who required a classic education.

The history of the school had been fraught with difficulties. After the Second World War and a period of exile, in 1945, the Franciscans returned to Bosnia. However it was not long before the student dormitory, built in the vicinity of the secondary school in 1928, was taken away from them and transformed into an army barracks; first for the Yugoslav Army and later up until December 2005, for the Federation Army.[2] The government closed the Franciscan school in 1946, but through the efforts of the provincial authorities the school opened once again in 1947, but only for Franciscan candidates. However, in

---

[1]Graeme, F. (tr.) <u>Franciscan Secondary School and Seminary in Visoko</u> (Franjevačka klasična gimnazija, Bosne Srebrene 4, BiH-71300 Visoko) 2008: page 5.
[2] Ibid., page 13.

accordance with the education reform from the 1950s, the secondary school had to accept a four-year school programme and so part of the secondary school was used as a state secondary school for twenty years.[3]   From 1947-1992 the Franciscan school (not the state school) with its eight year classical programme, was not recognised by the National government, creating difficulties for those who did not wish to study theology but wished to go to university or college. When the children completed their education, their diploma was not accepted by the universities; they were treated as if they were not qualified. However, in 1992, the school received its right to publicity and was then recognised fully.   From 1992-1996 the Franciscan secondary school was moved to Baška Voda on the Croatian coast, where the students settled into hotels offered to them by the Croatian government, safe from the many war dangers in Visoko.[4]

On several occasions, the Communist Government offered money to the Franciscans for the School, but the Franciscans would not sign the papers, saying that they would wait, one year, ten years, a hundred years; one day it would come back to them.

They will miss Florence; they say she lightened things and that she was cheerful, "gentle as a spider's web" (although she was never quite sure if this was a compliment) and that she laughed a lot.   For Florence, the Franciscans lightened and enlightened her. She was ashamed of her weariness when she saw how they had persevered, surmounting hostility, war, hunger, physical, emotional and intellectual difficulties over and over again.   She knew she would miss them, their courage and warmth, their openness and their affection.   She loved their

---

[3] Ibid., pages 13-14.
[4] Ibid., page 14.

monastery, their art, the decaying library, working in the garden where the roses seemed to come from Heaven itself. How she would miss going into the kitchen to be fed by the nuns with so much more than food. And those mountains that seemed to breathe, the mosques, the cafes, 80-year-old Sakib and all his stories and the language itself.

Fr Josip and one of the Sisters arrived with tea and biscuits for their visiting guests. Adem, who had the task of driving the group to the school, poured the Turkish coffee. The aroma swirled round the room in tantalising symphony.

> "We take all students" related Fr Josip, Muslims, Orthodox, Catholic, and now (he smiles) girls."

During the Bosnian war (1992-1995), Adem was conscripted into the army. He was 19 years old. His father also fought in the war and was wounded.

> "Who were you fighting?" he is asked. "Croatians" he replied. "I am a Bosnian Muslim, but we were all together; then we were fighting each other. We are all the same, Catholics and Muslims", he reflects. "It did not make sense but we had to do it; it was compulsory."

After the Bosnian War (1992-1995) the Franciscan seminarians returned to Visoko having been in Croatia and Dalmatia for four years during the war. The seminarians were happy to come back to their seminary school in Visoko and their neighbours were glad to see them. "The Franciscans have returned," they said; "all will be well now." They decided to open to everyone again but the army was still inside. In 2007 the Government handed the school back to the Franciscans, but only to use; they did not return the right of ownership.

> "It makes no difference to the Franciscans", reflects Fr Josip. "We had to respect the laws and agree to them. The grounds were returned to us only a few years ago, but only to use; it is not our property."

Many factions who had inhabited the building had left it in a very poor state of repair. The roof needed replacing and all the windows had been blown out with grenades from fighting soldiers. When first the soldiers came from the front line, they had the opportunity to destroy the building but because of reports that some refugees and nuns were inside, the school was protected. It was hard to remove the refugees when the school was returned to the Franciscans.

It was a difficult time during the war. A grenade from the Hills fell nearby. In the Library there were 70,000 volumes; very rare books, of both Muslim and Christian text, some hundreds of years old, but they were taken from the school one by one. All the neighbours helped to move the books and hid them, protecting them from being destroyed. No grenade hit directly on the building.

> "We were protected" recalls Fr Josip. "Two Franciscans were here, two Sisters from Slovenia: one was a gardener and they had lots and lots of salads, so much that she gave to the town and to the hospitals." [Laughter] "There were 80-85 students before the war but now there are only 45 students in the school."

Florence smiles at the visitors. She will miss her students with all their worries and tragic stories – Dajana, brilliant, gentle and with only nine fingers. Her brother chopped off the tenth. She is leaving, thank goodness, off to recover by studying Greek and Latin. Then Tijana, plagued by epilepsy, a sexually abusive grandfather and chronic bronchitis; the daughter of a prostitute and a drunk who froze to death one night. Martina, who surmounted the throes and razor blades of teenage depression wonders every day if her father, a 'de-miner', will come home alive from work. Laughing, she tells Florence not to worry. During the war he had put those mines there, so of course, he knows how to take them out. Senseless! The list goes on and on. But then there is dear, dear, Valentina, who speaks from the heart and is so full of hope. One of the few students from a stable family, whose father, with tears in his eyes, told Florence that they would do anything to get their daughter out of the country. "But then again, if she and all the young people go, where is Bosnia's future?" reflects Florence.

Florence knew in her heart that it was time to go and she knew that there was no more that she could do to help her students at Visoko. The flight to the U K seemed endless; emotion was an exhausting process that drained her last bit of energy. The university in Oxford welcomed her warmly as she arrived to sit the entrance test for advanced Ancient Slavik Studies. Her interview went well and the pain in her final goodbyes on her return to Visoko was lessened by the excitement and anticipation of a new beginning. England beckoned her and the next few years stretched ahead of her as an exciting roadmap of undiscovered treasures.

"How did you start to rebuild?" Fr Josip is asked.

He explained that repair to the damaged foundations cost €30,500 which was paid for by St Joseph & The Helpers Charity. During all the years of occupation, the basement area rooms were lowered without any additional stabilisation to the building. To alleviate concerns about this, a supporting wall was built around the perimeter of the building with damp proofing, cladding and drainage.

Arthur and the directors of the charity were brought to Visoko by Fr Mijo Dzolan the Franciscan Provincial at that time. Fr Josip recalls, "Arthur came to visit three or four times. To raise funds for restoration of Visoko, a pamphlet was printed and circulated and good people made donations.[5] Three or four years ago he came on St Patrick's Day. I recognised the Irish emblem on his jacket – a shamrock. I had Mass in English once a week and invited Arthur to the Mass. He did the readings for the Mass and was happy to celebrate with the students."

So, the initial phase was stabilising the building, installing hydro-isolation and drainage systems, fortifying walls and other construction. The remaining phases of the project were the demolition of the roof and walls down to the second level, building a new floor and putting on the new roof, including electrical installation, heating, plumbing, plant equipment, classrooms, dining and accommodation facilities. Some of the funds to cover the early reconstruction work at Visoko were received as follows:

- Ministry of Education, Science and Sport of Republic of Croatia - €303,315
- St Joseph & The Helpers Charity
  - €183,540
- Funds found by St Joseph & The Helpers Charity from a company trust in Dusseldorf - €190,000

---

[5]St Joseph & The Helpers Charity, Restoration and Modernisation of The Franciscan Secondary School at Visoko, Bosnia & Herzegovina. [Information on the project can be found at www.helperscharity.com].

Outstanding works, furnishing and equipping the school would cost in the region of €1,500,000 which Fr Mijo hoped to find in government grants and Trust donations. The Franciscan parishes and people of Bosnia and Herzegovina would help where possible.

Did you ever have any doubt that you would finish this project, Fr Josip?

"Yes, we first started the school which had no roof and three to four floors – it took more money than first thought. The students lived in guest houses and had their meals here – it was very cold. We hoped that it would be finished in three to four months, but it was really three to four years. It was just in 2008 when the students finally moved in. We had some doubts as the recession started and donations stopped coming in from Croatia. Then, of course after that we needed new furniture. The façade outside needs doing as it is losing heat and we need a Gym now. We have one but it is very small and very old."

"What could we do? We wrote applications, but we prayed; we prayed a lot. [Laughter]. That was when Arthur came. He had been visiting the Sisters at Kiseljak, helping them build a Kindergarten and so he came to visit us at the invitation of Fr Mijo. A plan was made for three phases; first the foundations at a cost of €30,500, then phase 2, to raise the building to accommodate an additional floor, replace the existing roof, put in new windows and floors, and pay for the brickwork, the cornices, the ventilation and guttering, that would cost €340,000. Then next was phase 3, where the heating, lighting, plumbing and plant

128

equipment would be installed and two classrooms, the dining facilities and accommodation for 30 students would be prepared.   That would cost €775,000."

It was a good feeling walking around the gardens. The visitors felt extremely relaxed.   The chickens were fat and content in their large open pen.   There were no pigs or cows anymore since it was not viable economically to raise pigs, but instead they grew rosemary and thyme.   The students sometimes worked in the gardens. Fr Josip points to the old army barracks site, affirming that that is where they will put their sports hall. The Army tanks were parked there during the Bosnian war. The dog was chained up, mainly to alert the Franciscans that someone might be attempting to steal copper from the school.

> "There had been a robbery at one time by two drug
> addicts. They attacked Fr Mijo. Others heard him
> and saved him from a serious assault.   We are safe
> here in Visoko; the police know us and the Mayor
> knows us and they came and asked at Christmas if
> we needed extra protection.   The dogs protect us."

One dog, a collie mix, was wary of the visitors, compliant at first and then agitated, protecting his food. The visitors move away.

> "What do you think about it here, Adem?"
> "It's nice", he replied.
> "You can send your daughter here for classical
> training when she is 15 years old. [smile].
> "Mmm, maybe" he responds.

> "Our library is open for all in the town." continues Fr
> Josip, "We have students coming here from the town. I

was a teacher in the town before I came and I helped the old people too. Fr Philips was very popular in maths. He helped me understand maths. Many policemen come to me in the street and say, 'we have learned from Fr Philips'. Step inside; I want to show you something interesting."

He holds the door open, the visitors step inside. The room does not hold the grandeur of St Bonaventure Monastery Church built into the school, the busyness of the kitchen, the airiness of the bedrooms or classrooms, or the comfort of the old Faculty library housing the rich collection of academic publications from the late nineteenth century. It it a room with glass display cabinets, and in each one, the most ancient of archaeological artefacts. The whole ambiance of the visit is one of interaction; Fr Josip takes great pride in showing the seminary and the school to the visitors, as well as the church, the kitchen the bedrooms, the classrooms, the library, the archaeological artefacts.

Three young Croatian people smile. They speak perfect English to the group. They respond to the questions. This impresses all concerned. A young man invites them to view his friend's room and then his room; also the computer lounge. He is proud of this wonderful establishment.

Donal invites the young man to view Arthur McCluskey on St Joseph & The Helpers charity website and explains about Arthur and his past life. Fr Josip is surprised. He did not know about Arthur's conversion and healing from gambling and alcohol and this is news to him. Arthur had always been very humble in their company.

Donal explains about the work of the charity and the young men listen intently.

"When he said 'Yes' to God," explains Donal, "he let God decide how he should live his life. God worked through Arthur and he was an instrument for God. It is God's amazing work; although he has died, the work will continue. Always the work continues."

Dario, only fifteen years old, explains that his wish had been to come to this school because this school is better than the most top school in Bosnia and Herzegovina. His problem was that he lived with his mother who lived 150 km from the school. The solution was for him to live at the school during the week but at the weekend to go home.

One young man explains that he studies sixteen subjects including five languages. He wants to be a doctor and can go to Zagreb or Sarajevo and study for five years or more. He cannot afford the university fees, but if he agrees to work at the school for a time, they will pay for his university degree. So, he will then come back to the school and teach subjects for two years.

It costs €260 per month to educate a young person at Visoko. There are day students but those who board can either go home at the weekend or stay at the school. There is study on a Saturday but plenty of free time to surf the internet and play basketball outside.
The students are enthusiastic, as education is a prize sought after by many young people in Bosnia and Herzegovina. Poverty and lack of work opportunities disables families and inhibits them from providing this necessary pathway to the future for their young. The Franciscan Secondary School and

131

Seminary in Visoko has become a beacon of light and hope to many, many young people.[6]

For a long time, the exterior of Visoko was in a very poor state of repair. It was of great concern as the bad weather could seriously damage all the good work that had been achieved inside the building. It was a great relief to the charity directors to hear that the work has now been done by a German Trust costing in the region of €250,000.

"Dear Mrs. Henry,

Thanks for your kind email. I have travelled to Visoko this April (2013) and visited the school as well. As far as I understood the renovation works should be finished by now. Back then only a minor part of the work was missing. So the school is fine for the moment, but of course they have plenty of plans and ideas for the future. Anyway I am quite confident that the existing premises are in good condition now.

Please find attached some pictures I took on that trip. You can see the last missing part of the renovation of the outside walls next to the entrance.

Best wishes and kind regards, Markus

---

[6] If you wish to contribute to the Franciscan School in Visoko, you can do so through:
St Joseph & The Helpers Charity, www.helperscharity.com or contact:
Pat Henry, Chairman (UK) at pat@helperscharity.com
Tel: +44 (0) 144239107 ; Mob: +44 (0) 7866224671 or
Donal O'Shea, Director (UK) at donal@helperscharity.com
Tel: +353 (0) 12858130; Mob. +353 (0) 872500424.

In May 28th, 2013, Fr Franjo Radaman, Franciscan School, Visoko wrote to Pat Henry, Chairman, St. Joseph & The Helpers (UK).

"Dear Pat

It is pleasure to hear You again a be sure that you didn't forget us. As you see. Our building has a new face. We finished it finally. In the next month it will be finished the fundament covered by stones and the entrance. Thanks be to God for so many people who are helping us. Situation in Europe and in Bosnia is still in bad economical position.

Our development must go on. We need and planning to start built new sport-hall ad sport camp. On the same time the old building (monastery) need to be permanently reconstructed. The Gymnasium is in both buildings. Let us hope to find some donators more who would understand our mission in this region.

Say hello to Sylvia and others people. I hope to have chance to visit Ireland and others centres of St Joseph.

May God and St. Francis bless all of you.

Fr. Franjo R"

2. John Paul II – Archdiocese Pastoral Centre for Youth, Pozivnica, Sarajevo.

The "Youth Centre" had been forming in Fr Šimo Maršic's mind for some time. His youthful exuberance complimented that of his Bishop's wisdom and experience as both sought to identify a solution to stop the young people leaving Bosnia and Herzegovina. The war from 1992-1995 had almost destroyed Sarajevo and the young priest realised that in a time of increasing political and economic difficulties the youth needed something more concrete, more substantial; a vision for the future, to entice them to stay and rebuild the country. Fr Simo and the Bishop saw the need to provide them with a perspective which would encourage them not to leave Bosnia and Herzegovina. The late pope John Paul II had built bridges between the people of various origins and religious convictions and this was never more urgent in the Balkans where surveys showed that in the future 60% of the young people, the "keepers of tomorrow" would leave Bosnia and Herzegovina, sooner rather than later.[7]

There were many obstacles to overcome. The "Siege of Sarajevo" had left deep-seated pain in the hearts of the population of 90% Muslims, 3% Serbs and 3% Croats. The young priest realised the importance of strengthening their Christian identity whilst at the same time intensifying the relationships with other ethnic groups. A Youth Centre would

---

[7]Letter from Dr. Šimo Maršic, Direktor Nadbiskupisjski centar za pastorl mladih Ivan Pavao II, Sarajevo, to St Joseph & The Helpers Charity Ltd, Ireland. "Subject: Construction of the Youth Center of the Archdiocese of Vrhbosna "John Paul II", dated, October 14th, 2010. Information relating to the Youth Centre has been retrieved from this letter with the permission of St Joseph & The Helpers Charity. In addition, during an interview in November 2012, Fr Simo related and confirmed the information to the author.

provide the ideal environment where young people could meet, be educated and grow in spirituality. Historically, Sarajevo had always been a meeting place. In the future it was hoped that Sarajevo and the whole of Bosnia and Herzegovina would be formally integrated into Europe.

It was therefore essential to work towards an integrated Bosnia and Herzegovina and the Youth Centre would enable that integration to take place at microcosmic level. It is generally accepted that education shapes the foundation of a country but in the broader sense of "personal development", understanding each other's religions, culture and traditions would enable the young people to develop sound competencies, formally, professionally and socially in order to spring confidently into the future, unhindered by the shackles of ignorance.

Fr Šimo knew that living in the city of Sarajevo, the young people would need to take ownership of the Youth Centre. In his opinion, by integrating and building relationships with each other, they would encounter "the hidden God" in each other and this would foster an active tolerance and acceptance towards each other, as well as every visitor to the centre.

Fr Šimo writes:

> "At the end of 2005, the Archdiocese of Vrhbosna, with the support of 'Renovabis' (a German Catholic Trust) bought a lot where a house was renovated and is currently used as the Youth Centre office, the office of the director of the Centre and a chapel. Besides the director, the Centre employs six full-time workers, around ten part-time workers and around fifty volunteers depending on the needs of the project.

There was a growing need for a larger facility in order to make our work and engagement with the youth more efficient and in order to continue developing new programs and initiatives. Therefore, in July 2011, we initiated building a Youth Centre, a place which will be the centre for encounters, education and spiritual development for the youth.

The building of the John Paul II Youth Centre will provide more office space, a place for workshops and seminars, a chapel, sport hall, space for various activities for the youth (music, dancing, drama club, art, media), a library, rooms for accommodating around fifty young people, a restaurant and a café."[8]

Although the Archdiocese of Sarajevo and thus the Catholic Community was instrumental in generating the funds and providing the vision to enable the building of the Youth Centre, Fr Šimo knew that he would need help from other organisations. On October 14th, 2010, he wrote to St Joseph & The Helpers, explaining the planned construction of the centre in phases and asking for their help.

It was a huge project and St Joseph & The Helpers had the greatest desire to help, but prudence and discernment was required in a country where there was so much need. The charity did not have the funds to donate the €250,000 hoped for by Fr Simo, even though this would be given over a period of three years. The directors of the charity had to consider what was their priority and how much could they comfortably ask their benefactors to provide? Arthur McCluskey and the

---

[8] Director, Rev. Šimo Maršić, Gatačka 18, 71000 Sarajevo, Bosna i Hercegovina. www.mladicentar.org

directors prayed.

Much work had already been done. The "old house" had been active since October 2005 when work began on the adaptation of the site. In May 2007, the Ministry of Justice in Bosnia and Herzegovina formally approved and recognised officially the Archdiocesan Youth Centre. Several young people operated from the old house, planning and co-ordinating activities, expressing feely their creative and inventive ideas. Their energy is infectious: clear skin, sparkling eyes, and wide grins as they greet their visitors to the building site which one day will be the Youth Centre; a meeting place focusing on peace, spiritual growth and education. The plans are self-explanatory. The Youth Centre will have accommodation for fifty young people, meeting rooms, computer rooms, a chapel and a gymnasium, and of course, a nuclear bunker as required by law.

Their excitement is obvious, even though this three million euro project seems nothing more than a dream. Already they have received more than three-quarters of the money they will require for the construction of the Centre. They have worked out that the running costs will be covered by people paying for the use of the gymnasium and by donations from the diocese. A clever plan to rent out parking spaces in the nuclear bunker area under the building will also generate much needed revenue. They also hoped that they would find sponsorship for students coming from poor families; approximately €675 per year or €75 per month for nine months of the year.

Five young women talk about the workshops they have organised, explaining what each project will mean to the individual and to society. The residential "Youth for Youth" project enables young people from all cultures and religions to integrate freely without the restrictions of curfews or time scales. They first recognised collectively that many elderly people live on their own in Sarajevo, often neglected by their families and past friends, and that there is a great need to support them with basic tasks. So the students decided to organise themselves into small groups and every week twenty students in four groups of five, visit approximately twenty old people in order to help them with housework, shopping, chopping wood, buying medication and taking them for a walk. The old people are so grateful, for this is the opportunity they need to talk, to chew over their feelings and fears with young people who may be Christian or Muslim or Serb Orthodox.

Many elderly people have no family to care for them and like other places throughout Europe, many are abandoned, unwanted, cast aside as having little to offer society. However, the young people reach out and cross the borders of generations, religion and ethnicity, embracing each unique individual with tenderness and wisdom, thus destroying the plague of loneliness, depression, despair, feelings of being worthless. Instead the old people experience love, laughter, concern and joy. Caring for the elderly stimulates the young person to contemplate the social and political structures within their society, an educational tool which will plant the seed of social change in the future.

The visitors are impressed. This is a monumental task, but they see it will work. One young student shows a visitor her new boots. "They are real leather" she proclaims proudly and the visitor smiles, noticing the high heels and frivolous decoration. They are fashion boots, just like all the other fashion boots worn by young people throughout the world, where fashion matters. It's refreshing to see that the same concerns, the same desires, exist in Sarajevo as elsewhere. This is hopeful, this is something to hang on to, that with time, there is a chance that normality will return to this bruised city. Normality, what does that mean for the Sarajevo community of today? The jobs are few and people are struggling to support their families. They know the importance of formal education and they are aware that they cannot give many of their young people that opportunity. Through the Centre many of them are given the opportunity to train in basic computer skills, enhancing their opportunity to find work.

The visitors are taken upstairs on top of the partially completed new Youth Centre. The cement structure is cold, uninviting, unlike the vision of what this will eventually be, but when they reach the top of the building, the panoramic view of Sarajevo is breathtaking. The minarets and turrets dominate and decorate the skyline, interspersed with one or two Christian crosses, reflecting their struggle for survival in a predominantly Muslim area. The young people are hopeful and with excitement they relate the benefits of the "The Summer Peace Camps" and the "The International Summer Camp" which allow them to talk freely about their feelings and fears with other young people. The Centre, although unfinished and in its embryonic stage, is already a hive of activity and will become even more so in the future. During the communist era, no work was allowed with the youth outside the perimeters of the church and already, there are many positive projects involving the young people of Sarajevo.

The young people wave goodbye to their visitors. It has been a fruitful visit, one which has illuminated the realities of this courageous, intelligent and compassionate generation. They do not complain; they do not look back. Their vision is to the future, their energy is directed to helping their country, finding a way on this difficult path to build, regenerate and live in peace. They are no different to any other young people throughout the world, except they are in the minority of those in Europe who have been faced with the realities and the atrocities of war. However, there is no apathy in their step, only a determination to walk forward and rebuild the shattered lives of their people. The visitors have nothing but admiration for this generation of young people of Sarajevo.

The Youth Centre will cost over €3,440,000 to build. St Joseph & The Helpers through the generosity of one kind benefactor has contributed €60,467 towards the building and €10,125 towards Educational Sponsorship funded by the Marian Conference in Irvine, California. For that, the young people are extremely grateful.

This brave plan led by Fr Šimo Maršic on behalf of Cardinal Puljic and the Bishops Conference of Bosnia and Herzegovina, is one which will integrate the youth, aid them to live and study in Sarajevo and Bosnia and Herzegovina, thus supporting them to remain in the country. This will furnish a Christian Catholic identity in the country and bring Bosnia and Herzegovina to a place of PEACE[9].

---

[9] If you wish to contribute to the Youth Centre in Sarajevo, you can do so through;
St Joseph & The Helpers Charity, www.helperscharity.com or contact:
Pat Henry, Chairman (UK) at pat@helperscharity.com
Tel: +44 (0) 144239107 ; Mob: +44 (0) 7866224671 or
Donal O'Shea, Director (UK) at donal@helperscharity.com
Tel: +353 (0) 12858130;   Mob. +353 (0) 872500424.

3. Education Funding

Perhaps it is difficult for people in Western Europe to appreciate fully the deprived structure of the Bosnian and Herzegovinian education system. We live in a society where education is a priority and an expectation, although often not appreciated fully. In time, Bosnia and Herzegovina will flourish, but it will take time, perhaps another twenty years from now in 2013. It is only by educating the young that the country has any hope of reaching a state of maturity, prosperity and peace.

- In 2011, St Joseph & The Helpers provided four new computers for a student hostel in Mostar.

- Tijana (see above) from Mostar is one of many students who cannot afford to complete their education or even commence their college education due to financial requirements in the family. Students like Tijana are worth supporting for they are hard working young people dedicated to gaining a formal diploma. In time, they will be able to support their siblings and help them with their education.

St Joseph & The Helpers is proud to be contributing to this goal but it is only through the generosity of those who have gained an education in the west that this can happen.

Chapter VIII

THE FINAL CHAPTER

When Arthur McCluskey came to Bosnia and Herzegovina he could have left with little or nothing, but God had a job to do in this special country and so He reached into His toolbox and found a tool that was perfect for the job; all God had to do was sharpen the tool and start work.[1] Touched by the Holy Spirit, Arthur reached out quietly and said, "What can I do to help?" There began a journey which would take him through the mine-strewn terrain of a weary Bosnia and Herzegovina and set him in the paths of broken families, orphaned children, physically and mentally debilitated young and old. In his asking, he prayed to His Father in Heaven, rolled up his sleeves and set to work and very soon St Joseph & The Helpers charity emerged and rose to play a positive part in the healing of Bosnia and Herzegovina. St Paul tells us that there are many gifts of the Spirit but the greatest of these is love.[2]

On 13th August 2011, Arthur left this world and set forth on his journey towards home and his Heavenly Father. His rucksack was light, with no material possessions, but having lived on the earth for 67 years, it was packed full of the most wonderful gifts he had accumulated to offer his Creator.

---

[1] McCluskey, A. My Healing from Gambling and Alcohol in Medjugorje (McCluskey, Monasterevin, 2004). The expression 'God's Tool Box' is a product of a spiritual illumination from Duncan Taylor in Aberdeen, Scotland.
[2] 1 Corinthians 13:13.

First, he took with him the gift of **INTEGRITY**, for Arthur had lived his life in truth and honesty as the Lord had wanted him to do; but it had not always been that way when, in his younger days, the world had led Arthur along the path of materialism, "integrity" had been placed in a top drawer marked, "to be used later if needed" and had been forgotten in the mists of time and the warm embalm of champagne and gambling. Had it not been for the prayers of his beautiful mother, the gift may have been forgotten entirely, but at the age of 55 years, his mother on Earth and his Mother in Heaven had had enough of his wild ways and with the prayers of one and the action of another, Arthur found himself in a little place in Bosnia and Herzegovina called Medjugorje.

Now Medjugorje did not have all the material attractions of Glasgow in Scotland, or indeed of Emo in Ireland, but it had something that Arthur could not escape – a lack of transport to the outside world. So trapped in the arms of Our Blessed Mother and an enthusiastic group of pilgrims, and one in particular called Nicky, Arthur could only escape to the hills. Since the hill furthest away from the village is Krizevac, known locally as 'Cross-Mountain', he found himself standing alone in front of a huge Cross which stretched out its arms, indicating, "STOP! NO ENTRY TO TRESPASSERS."

Several days later, having faced the ghosts of his hedonistic life and with the prospect of no entry to the Promised Land, he returned to the summit of Krizevac, placed both hands on the top of the altar incorporated into the base of the cross and with deep humility, love and contrition, bowed his head and whispered to his Lord, "Jesus, I am yours forever."[3]

---

[3]McCluskey, A. My Healing from Gambling and Alcohol in Medjugorje (McCluskey, Monasterevin, 2004).

The beginning of "forever" is never easy and stored in his rucksack to offer to his Lord was the gift of **COURAGE**, for it was at that moment when Arthur decided to change his life, that courage was needed to make amends to all those he had hurt and to admit openly that he was a changed man. Many rejected his promises of change, but armed with the gift of **FAITH** which the Lord had given to him, he pressed on with enthusiasm to complete the tasks which had been entrusted into his care; one of returning to Ireland in 1999 to care for his mother with the help of his siblings until she died in January 2002, and the other to set up a charity.

Now, the first task was pure joy to Arthur, for Arthur's mother was the teacher who taught him how to love unconditionally and he spent many happy hours with her praying the Rosary, but the second task required the gift of **COMMITMENT,** for this was to be used for the task that would become his life's work and would challenge him in ways which he had not contemplated. The Lord did not reject Arthur's past life but decided to use the knots and worn pieces and weave it into the tapestry of the future, for Arthur was one the shrewdest businessman known in God's Kingdom. Wrapped in the silken cobweb of experience, lying next to the gift of commitment in his rucksack, lay the gift of **WISDOM,** one of the gifts which he would use time and time again for the task ahead in Bosnia and Herzegovina.

He first embarked with the charity "Rebuild for Bosnia" and whilst he gained much needed experience in the life of the beautiful people of the Balkans, 'Wisdom' took him by the hand and led him to a Spiritual Director who would assist him in his prayer life to discern the Will of God. Soon Arthur became compelled to start a new charity and on May 19th, 2004, St Joseph & The Helpers Charity" was established with

144

the main objective of raising funds for the people of Bosnia and Herzegovina, to support them in rebuilding their broken lives after the 1992-1995 Yugoslav war.

Not knowing exactly how to start a charity, Arthur used his gift of **CHARM** and with his soft gentle Irish brogue, his twinkling eyes and his warm smile, soon he had gathered a group of Directors and Helpers to assist him with the task of launching the charity and gather the much needed funds to provide **HOPE** to the gentle people of the Balkans who were shattered by the conflict in their land.

Now at this point you might think that his rucksack was full to brimming but you would be wrong, for three gifts were sitting at the very top, for **HOPE** is not enough without **LOVE** and love is empty without **PRAYER and ACTION.** Daily, Arthur sat with His Jesus in the Blessed Sacrament and prayed quietly, asking the Lord to guide him, to keep him on the right path, whilst planning the next course of action. For Arthur loved the gentle people of the Balkans, the Franciscan Priests who had sacrificed everything for Jesus, the gentle Franciscan Sisters who with courage had stayed throughout the war to feed the people spiritually and physically; and he loved the most vulnerable of all, the orphans, the elderly, those who had been abandoned, abused; those who were haunted by the horrors of an unjust war.

And they loved him........ they loved his warmth, his laughter, his sense of fun, his love of life; they loved him, not for what he gave them, but for who he was; the man who said "Yes" to Our Blessed Lady and who refused to ignore the suffering in front of him. So stacked in his rucksack next to Love was the gift of **SUFFERING** for Arthur also understood the pain of suffering, he knew the pain of rejection, the pain of ridicule, the pain of being misunderstood, the pain of gossip, the pain of loneliness, and so the gift of **'suffering'** was a special gift, one that was given willingly, one that was given with pride.

In the middle of the gifts was the gift of his **TIME.** Arthur did not leave others to build the kindergarten at Kiseljak, but time and time again, visited the Sisters to work with them in ensuring the job was completed. His journeys took him to Visoko to help the Franciscans in rebuilding their decimated Secondary School. In the meantime he looked in on the newly appointed 29 year old Fr Slavisa Stavnjak who had arrived in Dezevice in the mountains to a leaking house, an arctic church and a dwindling ageing parish, to offer his support and practical financial help. He supported Sr Josipa and then Sister Kornelijie in repairing the John Paul II Orphanages at Citluk and Vionica and oversaw personally the building and the work of the Grandparents Home at Vionica, which provides a safe haven for the older generation who had lost so much during the war in Bosnia and Herzegovina. The new Community Centre (St Joseph's Hall) in Mother's Village, a product of Arthur and Fr Svet's determination and commitment emerged triumphantly; and he took time to listen carefully to the stories of those who had lost everything and without any trumpet of declaration, gave them his own personal financial support. In addition, with gentleness he encouraged those who were struggling to achieve their own tasks in Medjugorje and he took time to network for them, putting them in touch with the right people.

The gifts of **GENEROSITY and KINDNESS** balanced precariously on the top of his rucksack as he packed ready for the journey ahead. His many friends would miss this gentle giant, one who had a hidden streak of stubbornness and determination that could melt like the snow with a prodding gentle breeze of a child's laughter and understanding. The

146

charity 'Miracles' which provided limbs for those affected by the war, would weep at the loss of an avid supporter and friend, and the Sisters at Bijelo Polje would never have the opportunity to say "thank you" to him personally for the furniture donated to their new built kindergarten. Jane Dowd and the nurses from St Luke's Home Care charity would mourn at his passing and Lucija from Mostar would grow up unable to share her joy with the man who insisted on the new buggy that would enable her to participate in life freely. And the many children who benefited from his sponsorship programme would never have the opportunity to show him their graduation certificates.

But the time had come and although his family and friends would have liked him to stay a little longer, he was ready to go. He walked closely with Our Lord and he held Our Lady's hand tightly as he completed his tasks. Like Paul, he had "fought the good fight", "finished the race" and "kept the faith", and now the prize was his.[4] The rucksack was heavy, not with the wealth of the world, but with the wealth of Heaven, the gifts of **Integrity, Courage, Faith, Wisdom, Charm, Laughter, Hope, Prayer, Action, Suffering, Time, Generosity and Kindness** and everything that he had, he packed carefully to give to the Jesus who had stretched out His arms and drawn Him close, when Arthur had quietly whispered,

"Jesus, I am yours forever."

---

[4] 2 Timothy: 4:7.

APPENDIX I

TRIBUTES

"My Friend Arthur McCluskey: A Tribute"
By Wayne Weible[1]

From the moment we met, there was a predominant element of his personality that typified my dear Irish friend and brother in Christ, Arthur McCluskey, who passed away suddenly in August (2011) from a massive heart attack.   That one element was his profound humility. It personified his tireless effort to make up for time lost by living the message of Medjugorje by thought, word and deed to the best of his ability.

Arthur's spiritual conversion began when a relative invited him during a family wedding to come with her to Medjugorje. As he later described it, in a condition best described as "somewhat inebriated" from exuberant celebration during the matrimonial occasion, he accepted the invitation without a thought of actually fulfilling it.   After regaining his sobriety and exhausting every possible effort to get out of it, Arthur grudgingly made the pilgrimage to Medjugorje, determined to leave at the first opportunity.

The rest, as we say, is history. A man who made a fortune in business while losing himself in drink and gambling discovered

---

[1] Wayne Weible: Author and Speaker - www.medjugorjeweible.com
(Printed with permission from Wayne Weible, April 2013.)

the reality of God at the apparition site. Arthur McCluskey immediately gave his soul to God and his body to the work he was created to do. He became a prime example of living the messages the Virgin was giving to the world through Medjugorje.

I met Arthur in March 2000 during a two-week speaking tour organised by a group of Irish women. They had been to Medjugorje and witnessed the results of the horrible civil war that left the country in shambles. Inspired by the call of the Blessed Virgin's request to live Her messages, they wanted to raise funds to build homes for refugees in the war-torn country of Bosnia and Herzegovina, which is home to Medjugorje.

Patricia Keane, the head organiser of the tour, had given me on the day of my arrival a testimonial story of a successful businessman who suffered through years of addiction to gambling and drinking. His story convinced Patricia that he would be a wonderful addition to the tour. As she put it, he would be the "opening act" before my talks.

I sat at Patricia's kitchen table in her home early on the morning of our departure for the first speaking venue reading the story of this man's conversion. Suddenly, I felt a presence behind me and turned to see this rather tall Irishman standing there with this thick head of white hair bent down and his hands folded meekly in front of him. I stood to introduce myself to Arthur McCluskey. We shook hands and exchanged greetings but he hardly looked up muttering just above a whisper how overwhelmed he was to "meet such an icon of Medjugorje".

I laughed and replied to Arthur that I was just another convert like him and that I looked forward to our time together. After reading his testimony, I felt he would be an excellent addition to the tour.

At the opening speaking venue, Arthur gave his first public conversion witness, again with his head down and his hands folded in front of him. He barely spoke loud enough for the people to hear. Ten days later we were teasing him that now I was *his* warm-up act! He seemed to gather confidence with each stop of the tour and during that time, I gained one of the best friends of my life. The tour was the beginning of hundreds of talks of his conversion experience for Arthur.

A short time later, working with Patricia and Arthur for a newly formed charity named Rebuild for Bosnia, we raised enough funds to build more than 70 prefabricated homes for refugees in and around Medjugorje. Our friendship grew and soon Arthur began visiting my home in the states. We shared a love of the game of golf but mostly the work of Our Lady of Medjugorje.

After a while, Arthur felt called to start his own charity, which brought forth the organisation of St. Joseph & The Helpers. He asked me to be president of the charity in the United States and later its patron.[2] We worked together for the better part of nine years. Through his constant endeavour to raise donations, the Charity was able to build orphanages, retirement homes and school buildings among other things throughout the war-battered country of Bosnia and Herzegovina. It is Arthur's legacy.

---

[2] Unfortunately, inspite of Arthur's and Wayne's hope, due to government legislation, it became difficult to establish St Joseph & The Helpers Charity in the United States; however, donations can be made to the work of the charity in any currency. Please visit www.helperscharity.com and click to donate. PayPal will convert and deliver safely.

I grieved at the loss of such a wonderful friend after learning that Arthur had died at his desk just before leaving for an important engagement concerning the charity. He was due to visit us in October for a little golf and rest. Now he was gone. But soon my grief at the loss of such a good friend turned into absolute joy. I just knew in my heart that on his arrival at the gate of heaven Arthur had a sure fire guarantee of immediate admittance.

I am convinced that there was no purgatory time for this spiritually converted successful businessman. He pretty much covered that during his last years on earth, literally working to chronic exhaustion to establish and operate St. Joseph & The Helpers.. The result was that in just a matter of a few short years, the Charity raised millions in donations and accomplished enormous tasks of charitable deeds. Most importantly, he did even more by setting an example of living the message of Our Lady of Medjugorje.

In Arthur's sudden death I've lost a very dear friend and brother in Christ. But I rejoice in his victory. Thank you, Arthur, for your friendship and for your example of living the message of Medjugorje.

May the peace, grace and love of Jesus be with each of you.

In the Footsteps of St Paul

Raymond McGreevy

As we gradually attain maturity in life, subconsciously we develop our priorities. This is especially true of a true Christian. Life demands that we are in the world with worldly commitments but we must never neglect our obligations to the salvation of our immortal souls. Worldliness can become more relevant in our lives than Godliness if success comes our way or is achieved. This can be noted with regard to Arthur McCluskey's life and many others before they experienced the love of Our Blessed Mother in Medjugorje and conversion occurred.

Arthur's Pauline conversion during his first visit to Medjugorje contributed very much to my own interest initially. It was Arthur's Testimony, at the turn of this century, one night in Cavan with Wayne Weible (another Medjugorje convert) that confirmed my decision to go there. A man who had in the business world achieved all his worldly ambitions surrendered all to devote his life to the service of God.

His spiritual conversion on Mt. Krizevac was miraculous and instantaneous and his total commitment to Our Blessed Mother's wishes, as in Her messages, complete. Now he travelled the world giving Testimony of his conversion, evangelising, performing charitable works, especially in the war-torn country surrounding Medjugorje. What his charity, St Joseph & The Helpers achieved financially would be difficult to cover adequately; schools, kindergartens, houses for the homeless and dispossessed, orphanages and refuge in Mother's Village for many young people, a home for the elderly, to name just a few.

Today, few realise Arthur's total contribution to restoring some normality to this demoralised country of Bosnia and Herzegovina. He would always avoid public acclaim and worked only for the glory of God.

Rath De lena anam *(God rest his soul)*

Author's note:[3]

---

[3] Raymond McGreevy was instrumental in introducing Arthur McCluskey to the author, Sylvia Hoskins. Over the years, the three became very close friends. Raymond worked tirelessly to support Arthur in his charity.

A Tribute to Arthur McCluskey

Michael Douglas

The first time I heard Arthur McCluskey's name was in August 2006. My work colleague, Gerry Morgan, gave me an audio tape of Arthur's testimony which he had received from Fr. Aidan Carroll. As I sat and listened to Arthur's testimony it was evident that this man's heart had been truly touched on his first pilgrimage to Medjugorje. I could feel the humility and sincerity in his voice as I listened to his words. Arthur was a successful businessman who suffered for years with addiction to alcohol and gambling. Medjugorje had now changed all that and Arthur found a new addiction to Jesus and Our Blessed Mother. Arthur never gambled or took alcohol after his experience of Medjugorje.

My first encounter with Arthur was purely by accident. In July 2006, I had finished writing the first draft of my book "Medjugorje: Peace in My Heart".[4] This was my first attempt at writing a book and I was unsure how I should proceed from that point. For the next few weeks I pondered what I should do and it was at this point that I felt a great desire to return to Medjugorje. As this prompting grew, I somehow knew that if I returned to Medjugorje I would find the person who would help me to tie up the loose ends of my book; that is finding an editor and perhaps a publisher.

---

[4] Michael Douglas's books, "Medjugorje: Peace in My Heart" and "Medjugorje: The New Road to Damascus" can be bought at Mother's Village Shop in Medjugorje or by contacting the author on: m_douglas333@yahoo.ie or, telephone: + 353-18251655. Michael is available to give talks on his books.

I decided to travel to Medjugorje on Thursday 12th October 2006 and on arriving at Dubrovnik airport, found transport to Medjugorje and accommodation for the first night at Innes's house where I met two pilgrims, Sadie and Ger. On enquiring why I was in Medjugorje on my own and not with a group, I explained the situation about my book and explained that the book was about my spiritual journey in life and of other people who had found peace in their hearts on pilgrimage in Medjugorje. Sadie turned to me and said, "that man sitting across from us has a very good story; you should speak to him. His name is Arthur McCluskey".

I felt apprehensive at approaching a total stranger requesting help for my book, especially one who seemed to be well-known, but plucked up the courage and introduced myself. Although Arthur was busy, he took time to listen to my explanation about my book and how I needed to find an editor. I asked if he could help. He agreed to help and on the following Sunday after Mass I gave him a copy of the book to read. I believed it was God's providence that Arthur had been placed in my path.

Two weeks after I returned home to Ireland I contacted Arthur who gave me two email contacts and suggested I send a draft copy of my book to each one of them; one agreed to help me edit my book. Arthur and his friend, my wife Lily and I met at a hotel in Ireland to discuss the book and the outcome was positive. I wished to give all of the proceeds of the book to St Joseph & The Helpers Charity, since my only desire was to promote Medjugorje and help people find the peace I had found. At that point, Arthur offered to publish the book. Arthur had not only found me an editor, but he was offering to publish my book. Over the next few years, I learnt more about Arthur and the wonderful work he was doing for God: a kindergarten, old people's home, community centre and many, many more good works which Arthur achieved around Medjugorje and other parts of Bosnia and Herzegovina, all funded through his charity.

When I heard the news of Arthur's death, I was about to board a plane for Medjugorje and the first person I contacted was Arthur's dear friend who had helped me with the book.   I decided to carry on with my pilgrimage to Medjugorje and pray for Arthur's soul there where Fr. John and Fr. Paddy celebrated Holy Mass for Arthur, in Mother's Village.

Arthur, may your soul rest in peace and your spirit continue to shine in Medjugorje.

Praised be Jesus and Mary!

Michael Douglas.

A Tribute from:

Vesna Radisic and Sr. Dominika Anic; 17th August 2011

Dear Arthur,

You know that more than everything in the world we wanted to be with you today, to say the last goodbye to you as you go to your eternal resting place.

We wanted to be there with all those who loved and respected you. But we are sure that you know that circumstances made it impossible for us to come.

Words cannot express all the sorrow and emptiness we feel in our hearts, but at the same time we feel immense gratitude and pride that we were so blessed and honoured to have an opportunity to be the witnesses of the wonderful work of God which He did through you, especially everything you did for the children in the "St. Francis" kindergarten in Kiseljak.

Thank you for each and every step you took here in Medjugorje, because each one of those left a permanent and profound imprint in the hearts of the people that you met on the way. No matter if there were people who were telling you it was difficult and useless, you were still persistent in your belief. And, believe us, you chose the best way, and numerous are those who started to follow your example.

Your name and your heart which couldn't do anything else but love, and your hands which couldn't do anything else but give, will forever remain imprinted in the lives of many.

May God be your reward!

Until we meet again in eternity...

love,

Vesna Radisic and Sister Dominika Anic

From Sr. Jelenka,
Provincial of Franciscan Sisters,
to Arthur,
as he was laid to rest on August 17, 2011.

Dear Arthur,

What beautiful our last meeting was in Kiseljak June 25, this year. After that you wrote to me, "You could not believe that you would have such good time with Nuns-Sisters." We Sisters were with same feelings and for many days after your leaving for Medjugorje we were talking of you of your sense of humour and deep serenity, while you bade farewell, eight of us Sisters waving to you. We felt so blessed to welcome you, your sister Pat and your friend Susie. Remember when you said "goodbye till November" as if you wished to be with us a little longer.

Now here we are two Sisters in Ireland to escort you on your way to Eternity. Almighty God is encouraging us telling us: "That our life is changing but is not taken from us. Those who love God will be with HIM in HIS Kingdom. We strongly believe that you are with Him now and that you already had received the crown as good salary what you have done for His glory. Your good deed you have done for many people especially for us School Sisters of St. Francis of Mostar.

Restlessly you were inspiration to all of us toward love of Christ and His beloved Mother the Queen of Peace which nearness you felt so alive in your life. Transformation you have experienced in Medjugorje and Divine miraculous touch and grasp didn't give you peace any more. As ambassador of Our Lady you were so busy to work for Her. That miraculous peaceless to do more were your often pilgrimages to Medjugorje where you would fill your batteries to continue to witness God's love transforming it in to Exact way of good deeds. Who could count all your programs and charity activities nourished with financial and spiritual help? This was in St Joseph & Helpers Charity where you have been general motor to everything.

In Kiseljak, the kindergarten you have built five years ago exists because of your constant help. Thank you, our dear Arthur. On behalf of Our Community the Franciscan Sisters of Mostar and Kiseljak, again thank you. Our deep thanks goes to all the members of St. Joseph & Helpers Charity with only one promise that you are in our daily prayers in our Chapels especially one in Kiseljak where we have perpetual adoration.

Dear Arthur, thank you for your fervency to do good and at the same time your burning to do more. The foot prints of your generosity are behind you through all Bosnia & Herzegovina. You loved your Ireland but your second homeland was wounded Bosnia. Your home out of Ireland was in Medjugorje and Kiseljak as well. Love doesn't know the borders, in contrary erases them with deep prayer and hard work you witnessed the message of God's love throughout the world. That was our dear Arthur. In your letters you told us your desire to continue to do good quoting you "Keeping busy whilst there is some life in aging body."

When I informed one of the priests who often translated your letters to me and for me, that you have left us and died, he told me "I am sorry, his letters were a special one. He was wonderful man." You become close to Christ and that nearness changed not only your life but as well those you get in contact with.

You were so kind and generous human kind a good soul. You have taught us noble men live simple life, love a lot without selfishness, care with truth and the rest give to God. You study in Our Lady's school of love. You have taught and tutor others and us with your own example. You become an inspiration that carry's a sample message: our life is failure if it is not able to be an inspiration toward others on their way to God.

Dear Arthur, we are very sad and still don't believe this is real. While saying farewell to you, we wish to say THANK YOU! Thank you for your great love. Our thank you will become and remain prayer for you. Even though it is hard for us, we are happy; because good people do not die they only leave before us. We are happy because we know that love only changes vessel and shape and continues to live.

Dear Pat, dear relatives, co-workers and friends of our dear Arthur, on behalf of our Community School Sisters of Kiseljak and on behalf of myself, do accept our deep sympathy.

Someone said, "When some-one is coming to this world he or she alone cries, and when someone dies everyone cries and he or she alone laughs. Today while we are all crying our dear Arthur is laughing in the happiness where you do not know the end.

To you we are saying goodbye and we are sad because of your departure, but what we repeat in the Creed, we believe in the unity of saints, we believe in the resurrection of the body and we believe in the eternal life. We believe in resurrection.

May you rest in peace...Your Sisters from Kiseljak.

Sister Jelenka.[5]

---

[5] Letter from Sister Jelenka, Provincial of Franciscan Sisters, printed in original form of translation. Sr Jelenka and Sr Janja, accompanied by Fr Svetozar Kraljevic (Fr Svet), travelled from Bosnia Herzegovina to attend Arthur's funeral on August 17, 2011.

APPENDIX II

THE WORK CONTINUES..........

1. Kindergarten at Kiseljak

As there is limited state aid available, in order for the Kindergarten to survive, Arthur McCluskey pledged to the Franciscan Sisters that he would support the Kindergarten through his Charity by covering all maintenance, heating and lighting at a cost of €20,000 + each year. The Franciscan Sisters are extremely grateful for your support.

2. Kindergarten at Bijele Polje

Many little children in the area need sponsorship to attend this wonderful kindergarten. Sponsoring a child's education at this stage in their life is a satisfying way to contribute to building the future of Bosnia and Herzegovina.

3. The Priests

There are many parishes and many priests who are urgently in need of support. Many are living in dilapidated parish houses and many of the churches are without basic needs such as heating, a costly commodity in Bosnia and Herzegovina.

4. Mother's Village

Mother's Village Orphanage was started in 1993 by Fr Slavko Barbaric helped by the Franciscan Sisters. It evolved out of the need for protection and care of the children who had lost both their parents and their home during the war. Today, there are over 50 children living at Mother's Village who need help with food, shoes, clothes and education. Buying goods locally helps the economy and we therefore appeal for financial support for the children at Mother's Village.

With your help, the Charity has built a Community/Sports Centre called St Joseph's Hall in the grounds of Mother's Village Orphanage. It is proving to be a great asset and is available to the local community and schools. The Hall is regularly used by the children and the 30 young men who are on a drug rehabilitation programme at the Village. The sports flooring was expensive and is well looked after by the staff. The Hall is used for celebrating Mass for pilgrims to Medjugorje on special occasions as it can accommodate up to 2,000 people. It is also used for concerts like the one organised by the charity on 2nd July 2013. James Kilbane, an Irish singer from Achill Island, Melinda Dumitrescu, the wonderful Romanian violinist we hear at St James Church's liturgies, Carmel Horan and Barry McCarthy, who provide the music at English Masses, and excellent local musicians performed to around 600 people raising almost €6,000 for Mother's Village. Ivan Mikulic, who sang for Croatia in the Eurovision Song Contest, caused great excitement and even the Medjugorje guides were dancing in the aisles! The event provided an occasion to say farewell to Fr Svetozar Kraljevic before his departure to a seminary at Zagreb.

A chapel is being developed upstairs at the rear of St Joseph's Hall and the space underneath will provide much needed secure storage for lawnmowers and other gardening and sporting equipment. There are now four bedrooms available for visitors and hundreds of young people sleep in the Hall during Youth Week.

5. John Paul II, Nos 1 and 2, in Citluk and Vionica.

The orphanages have provided a vital life-line for the children and will continue to do so for the foreseeable future. Many social problems in Bosnia and Herzegovina ensure that orphanages continue to be needed for the protection and care of children. With limited state aid available, the orphanages rely on donations to survive.

6. Children such as Little Lucija

Handicapped children are often forgotten in the drive to sustain the thousands of other children who need help. Many children like little Lucija are secure in a loving home, but there is no money available to buy special equipment, like a wheelchair, which can open that child to a new world. Help is much needed to support the many handicapped children in Bosnia and Herzegovina.

7. Mothers such as Ornella.

The country is still trying to develop its medical support many years after the Bosnian war finished. It is difficult to find a medical facility that would provide neurological care for someone such as Ornella. Ornella is only one tragic victim, but until medical facilities are built, which requires funding, care at home is the only means of ensuring round the clock care. However, it takes substantial financial support to provide the facilities to enable a Mother such as Ornella to be cared for at home.

8. Fathers, like 'Shovel' who wish to support their Families.

Shovel, a loving committed man who supported his family as best he could is one of many men who stand on the corner streets hoping that someone will give them one day's work. The effect on the man and also on the family is difficult to imagine if work is not forthcoming. Donating basic tools or a car or van to a self-employed worker is providing a future for an entire family. There are many "Shovels" the charity would love to support.

9. The Widow who has no means of support except through charity.

Unlike the countries in the European Union, there is no widow's pension and limited means of support for a young woman with children. Widows are vulnerable and are often taken advantage of by others in society. Please think about helping a widow to support her children.

10. The Grandparent's Home, Vionica

This lovely Nursing Home stands in the grounds of Vionica Orphanage, a few kilometres from Medjugorje. Over 30 elderly residents live at the Home where they are cared for with love and respect. When Irish or UK pilgrims visit the Home, they are warmly welcomed as the residents know that they support them. A loving hug is a comfort to these people who have lost so much. One old lady, through an interpreter said: "Thank you from the bottom of my heart. Without you we would not be alive. I was not always like this; I used to have a home and family." The sad reality is that the cruel war of '92 – '95 destroyed families and communities. Almost a whole

4

generation was wiped out leaving the older generation without support.

The original concept behind this building was that it would house the grandparents of the children in the orphanage. Sadly, those children had lost all their parents during the dark days of the Yugoslav wars. Not one mother or father of the children at Vionica orphanage survived the atrocities. Some of the grandparents are still alive and are happy to be living in clean, comfortable surroundings. They are well fed and cared for and there are medical facilities on the premises should they become ill. Some of the elderly people from a nearby refugee camp are now being accommodated at the Home too. They had lived for years in tin huts and had to queue for food, water and toilet facilities.

They continue to need our support and are totally dependent on charity to survive.

11. St Luke's Home Care, Medjugorje.

St Luke's Home Care is led by Jane Dowd, an Educational Health Nurse, from Co Galway, Ireland. Jane now employs four local nurses with their irreplaceable knowledge of both culture and language. Formerly unemployed, these dedicated professionals are making a huge difference in the lives of people of all age groups who were traumatised because of war and ethnic cleansing. The incidence of poor health, even among the young, is very high. As there is limited local infrastructure to cope, St. Joseph & The Helpers is very happy to support Jane and her team in providing care. The Charity donates €10,000 per year to fund a salary, car expenses and medicines for one of Jane's nurses. With your help we can provide much needed resources for Jane to enable her to fund and expand this programme of care in the community.

12.   The Miracles Centre for Prosthesis and Care, near Mostar

The Miracles Centre for prosthesis and care was completed in May 2009. The aim of making one limb a week in the first year is ahead of target. However, thousands are waiting in hope for a new or replacement limb so your support is needed for these damaged people. There is no government provision of limbs for amputees.

Bosnia and Herzegovina is still one of the seven most land mined countries in the world with an estimated 500,000 mines still to be cleared in 2013. There have been 1,660 victims since the war ended in 1995 of whom 328 (20%) are children. Children need their prosthetics altered or remade every six months to accommodate growth. Without this regular support their prosthetic limbs become useless. Children as young as ten years of age require replacement limbs as they grow and there is a long waiting list for such treatment and care.

13. Respite   Centre   for   Special   Needs   - Tomislavgrad

Mr Ivan Vukadin, the Mayor of Tomislavgrad, asked the charity for help to complete a School/Respite Centre for children and young adults with Special Needs. The shell of the building was up but work ceased in 2012 due to lack of funds. This facility is now completed and functioning but there is a great need to support the families and help the children to reach their full potential, through the provision of specialist equipment. In time, it is hoped to extend the Respite Centre to accommodate even more children and young adults with Special Needs.

14. Pastoral Centre and Public Kitchen, Dobrinja, Sarajevo

In the area of Dobrinja a food kitchen has operated from the Bosnian war days, when people of good will tried to save the lives of a starving population. After the war, the kitchen worked in a war shelter. This is one of four kitchens of "The Bread St. Anthony"; two are in Sarajevo, one in Mostar and one in Vares with over 1,000 meals provided and many delivered daily. "The Bread of St. Anthony", (Kruh sv Ante) is a Franciscan Charity which feeds the poor of all nationalities and their number is growing from day to day.

15. Franciscan School, Visoko

Built in 1900, Visoko school was the most prestigious Secondary School in Bosnia & Herzegovina and open to all religious groups. In 1945 the Communist Party confiscated the building and adjoining grounds for occupation by The Yugoslavian National Army. This arrangement continued until the fall of communism in 1992 when the Bosnian Army took possession. The building was handed back to the Franciscans in 2007.

The interior of the building has been restored and the school has been fully operational for the past few years. Funds are still needed to develop the Library as most of the books were destroyed by the Communists and the war. Resources are urgently needed for the Language and Science Laboratories and donations to develop indoor and outdoor sporting facilities would be gratefully received.

14. John Paul II – Archdiocese Pastoral Center for Youth, Pozivnica, Sarajevo

This dynamic centre is a beacon of light in Sarajevo. Many people in the community are being helped because of the enterprising and innovative youth programmes which are currently on offer and will eventually be undertaken in this building.

The construction is ongoing and Fr. Šimo Maršic and the young people require over €1,400,000 to complete the project. They are asking for your help in any small way whatsoever.

15. Student sponsorship

St. Joseph & The Helpers view education as one of the most effective ways of helping families escape from poverty and deprivation. If they cannot have access to some form of education, what future is there for them?

The charity has been asked to provide sponsorship for students who come from deprived backgrounds, whose families cannot afford the cost of the college fees. The charity sponsors a number of students in colleges in Mostar. Currently they pay €1,000 per year for a student who lives at home. However, it costs the charity €2,600 for students who have to pay for accommodation, food, fees, transport and books. The charity appreciates your support in giving a student hope for a better future.

16. Family Support

Poor families are regularly brought to the Charity's attention, mainly by Sr Jelenka from the Kindergarten at Kiseljak. They can only help if they have funds available and currently the Charity is helping a number of families with monthly payments of €100. The welfare system is almost non-existent in Bosnia and Herzegovina and only the poorest of the poor qualify for a welfare benefit of €40 per month.

Each Christmas St Joseph & The Helpers has traditionally sent €1,500 to Sr Jelenka to help poor families and they are most grateful for the support. Some families need help with day to day living but others are in need of a home. In spite of huge efforts to repatriate them, there are still thousands of people living as refugees having been ethnically cleansed during the war. They have no home apart from a hut with a tin roof in a refugee camp.

Arthur's death is not the end of the charity. It was his wish to ensure that the work continued in the event of his death and he set up the charity with a group of directors entrusted with the role of helping and supporting the people of Bosnia and Herzegovina.

Many people asked Arthur why St Joseph & The Helpers Charity did not support people in Ireland or the United Kingdom. His answer was simple. He said,

"In Ireland, the UK and the USA there are many charities; many support systems and government help to support the poorest of the poor. In Bosnia and Herzegovina there is limited support and many people are dependent on the help of outsiders to survive. That is why we must help our brothers and sisters in Bosnia and Herzegovina. That is why St Joseph & The Helpers Charity was formed; to help the people of Bosnia and Herzegovina." No amount of help is too small.

- If you are a **UK tax payer**: Gift aid adds 25% to every donation.

- In **Ireland**: a Charity can claim tax relief of 31% on an individual's donations that exceed €250 in a year.

The directors of St Joseph & The Helpers Charity personally cover all administration costs so that 100% of all donations benefit the people of Bosnia and Herzegovina. If you wish to support any of the projects in Bosnia and Herzegovina by contributing financially or would like to discuss any one of the projects with a Director, please do so in the following way:

Through the website: **www.helperscharity.com**

Pat Henry, Chairman (UK)

> **E-mail:** pat@helperscharity.com
> Telephone: +44 (0) 144239107
> Mobile: +44 (0) 7866224671

Donal O'Shea, Director (UK)

> **E-mail:** donal@helperscharity.com
> Telephone: +353 (0) 12858130
> Mobile: +353 (0) 872500424

Appendix III

Proceeds from the Sale of The Book,

Dear Arthur: The Fruits of Your Labour

by

Sylvia Anne Hoskins

will be donated to

St. Joseph & The Helpers Charity (UK)

....